Honest Rituals,
Honest Sacraments

Honest Rituals, Honest Sacraments

Letting Go of Doctrines and Celebrating What's Real

JOSEPH MARTOS

RESOURCE *Publications* · Eugene, Oregon

HONEST RITUALS, HONEST SACRAMENTS
Letting Go of Doctrines and Celebrating What's Real

Resource Publications
An Imprint of Wipf and Stock Publishers
199 W. 8th Ave., Suite 3
Eugene, OR 97401

www.wipfandstock.com

PAPERBACK ISBN: 978-1-5326-4045-2
HARDCOVER ISBN: 978-1-5326-4046-9
EBOOK ISBN: 978-1-5326-4047-6

Manufactured in the U.S.A.   11/21/17

All scripture translations are mine except those marked NABRE = The New American Bible, Revised Edition.

Excerpts from the Rite of Baptism and the Rite of Confirmation are taken from *The Rites of The Catholic Church as Revised by the Second Vatican* Council (New York: Pueblo Publishing Company, 1976)

To Arden, my wife of twenty-five years
and hopefully many more.
Our life together has helped me to understand
what is symbolic and what is real.

Contents

Preface

I NEVER INTENDED TO become an expert on sacraments.

As a college philosophy major, I had always been interested in epistemology, which investigates the problem of knowledge. How do we know what's real? How do we tell truth from falsehood? How do I know that life is not an illusion? Could I be asleep and dreaming that I am awake?

Even when I was a seminarian in Rome, questions about knowledge continued to bother me. How do I know that what we believe is real? How much of the Bible is fact and how much is fiction? What if the Protestants were right and the Catholics were wrong?

Fortunately, some of my fellow students told me about a Canadian Jesuit who was teaching at the Gregorian University at the time. His name was Bernard Lonergan, and although I never had him as a teacher, a book he wrote helped me to answer many of my questions. Reading *Insight: A Study of Human Understanding* over and over helped me to understand the workings of my own mind and, by extension, how human beings come to know what they call reality.

After leaving the seminary, I earned a Ph.D. in philosophy, but I couldn't find a job teaching. In the 1970s the baby boom was over, and schools were laying off teachers rather than hiring them. This was also shortly after Vatican II, and the field of religious education was opening up as women in religious orders moved into other forms of ministry. Shortly after graduation, I was hired to direct the religious education programs in a parish outside of Chicago.

A few years later, I landed a job in a small college in Iowa that needed a philosophy teacher and a theology teacher but could not afford to hire two people. With my background in both fields, I was able to meet their need and they were able to save money. Moreover, since I had been in charge of sacrament preparation programs in a parish, they asked me to teach courses on the sacraments.

To my dismay, all the books available reflected pre-Vatican II sacramental theology except the ones written by scholars for an academic audience—too difficult for college students. My experience in the parish told me, however, that the best approach to sacraments for an adult audience was a historical approach, one that showed how sacramental practices had changed over the centuries and that also showed how Catholic doctrine on the sacraments had developed over time.

It was to fill a need, therefore, that I wrote *Doors to the Sacred: A Historical Approach to Sacraments in the Catholic Church*, which was first published in 1981. Shortly after that, good books on the sacraments written for a general audience began to become more plentiful, but *Doors to the Sacred* remained popular, so I updated it with new material every ten years or so. My second book, titled simply *The Catholic Sacraments*, was an introductory volume to a set of books on each of the seven sacraments. In it, I tried to articulate the frame of reference within which I situated the history of the sacraments and their theology when writing *Doors to the Sacred*. Being part of a set, it never sold well on its own, but I was able to expand it and bring it into the digital age with a website that illustrated the variety of sacramental practices in Catholic, Protestant and Orthodox churches. *The Sacraments: An Interdisciplinary and Interactive Study* appeared in 2009.

When researching *Doors to the Sacred*, it became clear to me that Catholics talk about sacraments in a way that other Christians do not. In particular, we talk about administering and receiving sacraments. Obviously, such language is appropriate when speaking about the Eucharist, but what about the other sacraments? We talk about receiving the sacrament of confirmation, and when we say that we are not talking about the oil that is received on the forehead. We talk about receiving the sacrament of penance although nothing physical is given or received. We talk about receiving the sacrament of matrimony, the sacrament of holy orders, and the sacrament of anointing in the same way. This manner of speaking suggests that something invisible is being given and received through the performance of the visible rite.

The philosopher in me wanted to understand where this belief came from. Why did we Catholics believe this when other Christians did not? How well grounded was this aspect of our faith?

To answer those questions, I had to look more closely at the history of sacramental theology than did the earlier scholars on whom I relied when writing *Doors to the Sacred*. A few years ago, I found out that all of the historical documents I needed had been digitized. If I had wanted to look for the answers in 1981, it would have taken decades of reading original works in Greek and Latin. Doing the research in the digital age with a computerized word search program, it took only a couple of years.

The results of that research were published not long ago under the title, *Deconstructing Sacramental Theology and Reconstructing Catholic Ritual*. With such a long title, the book needed no subtitle! But with almost 900 footnotes, many in Greek and Latin, it was not a book that could be read by the average Catholic.

The present book attempts to put into ordinary language the results of that scholarly work and its implications for Catholic liturgical life. Whereas the former book was written to prove something, this one attempts to persuade.

Introduction

BILL AND SARAH WERE married for three years when his Army reserve unit was called up for a tour of duty in Iraq. While stationed there, Bill saw a number of his buddies blown up by roadside bombs—what the Army called improvised explosive devices or IEDs. Although he himself was not severely injured, he was discharged after 13 months with what used to be called shell shock but is now called post-traumatic stress disorder, or PTSD.

Although Bill tried to pick up his life where he had left it, he got fired from his old job and was not able to keep another one for more than a couple of weeks. He wanted to be a husband to Sarah, and he tried to be a father to the daughter who was born just before he was deployed, but his emotions were blocked. It was as though he wanted to feel something for them, but something inside kept him from making any personal attachments. Whenever he tried to reach out emotionally, the pain of loss prevented him from moving from thought to action.

One day Bill disappeared, and some months later one of his Army friends phoned Sarah to tell her that he had found Bill living in a homeless encampment in a different state. Despite his friend's best efforts, however, Bill could not be persuaded to return home, and he did not want Sarah to know where he was.

Some time later, Sarah fell in love with a different man. She wanted to marry him but, being Catholic, she could not divorce and remarry without getting an annulment. There was no way to find Bill, and her parish priest, who had known them both, doubted that she had grounds for an annulment. According to Catholic theology, she and Bill were still married unless it could be proven to a church court that the marriage was somehow defective from the very beginning.

Eventually she divorced Bill and remarried, not in a Catholic church but in a Methodist church that was more accepting of people who had experienced the agony of marital breakdown.

∗

Theresa, or Terry as she was known to her friends, had been raised Catholic, but her parents were not particularly devout, and when she went away to college, she dropped out of religion altogether. In her junior year, she took up yoga and for a while she thought she might be attracted to Hinduism. But then she joined a meditation group and felt a much greater spiritual kinship with Buddhism, since it was a religion that did not talk about God but emphasized peace in one's inner life and compassion toward others. After practicing meditation for a number of years and reading Buddhist literature, she felt comfortable identifying herself as a Buddhist even though she never became affiliated with any particular Buddhist sect. After a few years, she changed her first name to Tashi since it was close to her original nickname.

The only one who worried about Theresa's salvation was her grandmother. In her mind, Theresa's soul had been stamped with an indelible seal when she was baptized, and it identified her as belonging to Christ forever. Now that Theresa had given up her faith, she was in a state of mortal sin, meaning that when she died, her soul would go to hell. Theresa might think she is a Buddhist, but the seal of baptism made her a Christian forever, regardless what she called herself. Every day her grandmother prayed that Theresa would come back to the faith before she died.

∗

His parents had made a great financial sacrifice to send Ted to a Catholic high school, but even though he had a religion course every semester, there were still some things about his religion that did not make sense to him. Years ago, when he was preparing for his first communion, he was told that the bread and wine were the body and blood of Christ—something that seemed like magic to him when he was in the second grade, but he accepted it because he trusted his teachers. They also said that Christ was really present in the Eucharist, but now that he was older, he was beginning to have his doubts. To him, communion just seemed like bread and wine, and the mass was just a weekly ritual that Catholics went through.

Before Ted made his first communion, he had been taught to go to confession. They had made a big deal of it, but since then no one talked about it. At first it seemed like going to confession before communion was important, but now everyone went to communion without bothering with confession. Why was that? Having to tell your sins to a priest in order to have them forgiven just didn't make sense. And besides, what was a sin these days?

✶

Brenda was apprehensive about being appointed religious education director in her parish, which had been without one for a year. Numbers in old St. Patrick's parish had been declining for some time, and when the previous director had left for a better paying job, the parish council decided to leave the position open and hire someone part-time the following year. Now the year was up, and Brenda was expected to move the program forward.

Father Murphy had suggested introducing a Children's Word program—taking children out of Sunday mass before the readings and bringing them back after the homily. With only a small number of grade school children left in the parish (including Brenda's own), they could be divided into three groups and given lessons that were age-appropriate instead of having to sit through the adult liturgy.

Brenda's job was mainly working with the parent catechists once a month, providing lesson plans but also exposing them to a certain amount of adult faith formation—Bible study, Catholic doctrine, and the importance of Vatican II, which was ancient history to the young parents in the program. But she also had to work directly with the children who were preparing for their first celebration of the sacraments.

First confession and first communion were fairly easy to get through because the children were so young that they accepted what they were taught without question. Confirmation was a different matter, though. The teenagers in her little class, including her own son Jack, seemed totally bored by the idea of having to go through another church ritual. What difference did it make, anyway? Telling them that they were going to become adult members of the Church rang hollow even in Brenda's mind, since she knew that the older they got the more likely it was that they would stop coming to mass.

There was some talk in the diocese about moving confirmation to before first communion, something about the proper order of the sacraments of initiation. Maybe that would make her job easier. The kids were so much more docile when they were still very young.

*

Carla and José were active members of their growing Texas parish. The influx of migrants, both legal and undocumented, presented opportunities as well as challenges for parish ministry. Hispanics and Anglos worked well together under the guidance of Father Garcia and a multicultural parish council. The mass on Saturday and the three on Sunday were always full, and there were so many musicians in the parish that it was easy to find talented people to play instruments and lead the singing during the liturgy.

The main problem was not enough priests! The bishop was doing all he could to import priests from other countries—mainly Mexico and India, but also some from Vietnam, since there was a sizeable Vietnamese presence in the diocese. All of the masses got said, but who could understand what those foreign priests were saying? Ordaining deacons from among the men in the parish solved some of the problem since their homilies in English or Spanish were generally understandable. But the rest of the liturgy—it might as well be in Latin!

And then there was the ministry to the sick. Carla was a hospital chaplain, and José brought communion to shut-ins, but there were many people who could not receive the anointing of the sick when it was offered at the special liturgy held on weekday mornings. Carla was always being asked when a priest might come, but most of the time all she could do was rest her hand on the patient's head and offer a prayer for healing. She often left the hospital asking herself why only a priest could anoint the sick.

*

Roger had not been raised a Catholic, but when he fell in love with JoAnne, they talked about getting married in the Catholic Church. She was an active member of her parish, and she knew that it had a popular RCIA program for people who wanted to learn more about the Catholic faith.

The Rite of Christian Initiation of Adults was originally designed for use by missionaries to instruct non-Christians who wanted to join the Catholic Church. More than a single rite or ceremony, it was actually an introduction to Christianity that used a combination of instruction, personal faith sharing and liturgical rituals designed to move initiates from first inquiry to full membership in the Church. The whole process could take up to three years, culminating in baptism and confirmation at the Easter Vigil.

In the United States, however, the program had been adapted for people who had been baptized in another church but who wanted to become Catholics. Most were simply confirmed in the Church during the final ceremony, but those who had never been baptized before received that sacrament as well.

About half way through the program, Roger was informed that there was going to be a problem. He had been married and divorced long before he had met JoAnne, but before he could be married in the Catholic Church, he would have to have his first marriage annulled. Roger was confused. Why wasn't his divorce good enough?

The parish priest explained that God had made marriage indissoluble, so in the eyes of the Church he was still married to his first wife. Unless it could be shown that his first marriage was not a true marriage from the very outset, he could not get an annulment and be married to JoAnne in the Catholic Church.

Roger thought the priest's explanation was silly and stupid. It would be dishonest, he believed, to say that his first marriage had not been a good one at the beginning. He and Sheila had been very much in love, but they were also young, and in time they simply grew apart. The separation had been amicable and the divorce was by mutual agreement.

So Roger became a Catholic, but he and JoAnne were married in a civil ceremony. To make it easier for her, they joined a growing parish on the other side of town, where they had bought a new home. No one asked if they had been married before, and they saw no reason to tell anyone, either. As far as the pastor was concerned, they were just new members of the parish.

✶

None of these stories make religious sense, and some of them are examples of ritual dishonesty. Questions abound. Why would a religion in the twenty-first century say that marriage is indissoluble when it is clearly not? Why would anyone say that the effects of baptism are permanent when clearly they are not? Why do Catholics still have rituals like confession and confirmation when they do not seem to have any purpose? Why do the marriage rules of the Catholic Church force some people out and make other people hide their marital status? Why can't the Catholic Church have married priests or women priests or even simply more priests? What's so special about priests that they are needed to preside at the liturgy and to anoint the sick?

The basic reason is that Catholicism is trying to be a contemporary religion while hanging on to medieval ideas. Although we Catholics rightly believe that our faith goes all the way back to Jesus and the apostles, many aspects of our church life go back only to the twelfth and thirteenth centuries. Older Catholics know that the old beliefs and rules worked pretty well until the middle of the twentieth century. The mass was in Latin, priests were plentiful, Catholics hardly ever divorced, people went to confession before going to communion, confirmation made sense, and anointing of the sick (then called extreme unction) was always available to those who were dying. Those who were baptized in the Church stayed Catholics for life, and the men who were ordained remained priests forever.

Something happened during and after the Second Vatican Council (1962–65) that changed all this. Pope John XXIII called for an *aggiornamento* or updating of the Catholic Church, and most Catholics welcomed the change as long overdue. Changing the eucharistic liturgy and other sacramental rituals, however, had unintended consequences. The mass in English did not support the experience of Christ's presence in the Eucharist the way the mass in Latin had. Moral theologians used the findings of psychology and sociology to develop a more sophisticated understanding of sin and forgiveness, leading many to stop going to confession on a regular basis. Liturgical theologians used historical studies to encourage greater lay participation in the mass, including the use of more contemporary music. Scripture scholars urged Catholics to read the Bible for a greater appreciation of the Judeo-Christian tradition and to deepen their own personal spirituality. Some conservative Catholics saw the changes as a betrayal of the Church's tradition, as the once unified institution splintered into a bewildering array of regional and ethnic differences. Even liberal Catholics admit that what happened after the Council was much more than was envisioned by the bishops who attended the Council.

One thing that did not change very much was Catholic sacramental doctrine and the religious rules based on that doctrine. If you look at the 1983 Code of Canon Law or the 1994 Catechism of the Catholic Church, you will see that much changed around the edges, but the basic teachings and rules remained the same. That's why bishops were not allowed to use the rite of reconciliation for pastoral reasons when there were not enough priests to hear individual confessions. That's why the above stories are based on actual experiences. That's why the prayers used at Mass were retranslated in 2011 to make them sound more like the Latin prayers on which they are based.

How did a world-wide church with over a billion members get into this situation? Why has an institution with a long and deep intellectual tradition failed to understand what is happening to it today? Why is it stuck in a medieval mindset that makes its religious rituals so dysfunctional?

There is much more to the situation than what can be said about the sacraments. But looking at symbols and rituals from a non-theological perspective can provide some insight into the origins of the impasse and suggest some ways around it.

1

Symbols and Meaning

IMAGINE YOUR LIFE AS a robot.

With your camera eye, you could see what you are looking at. And with your microphone ear you could hear any sounds in your vicinity.

The difference is that you would not know what you were looking at, any more than a camera does. Nor would you understand what you are hearing, any more than a listening device does.

Ordinarily, we do not allude to the fact that we understand what we are seeing, and that we comprehend what we are hearing. There are exceptions to this, of course.

You might go into a museum and see a piece of abstract art on the wall, and you ask, "What is that?" Of course, you understand that it is a painting, but beyond that, what you are seeing is meaningless to you.

Similarly, your car might stop running, so you get out and lift up the hood, but when you do, all you see is a jumble of mechanical parts. You understand that they are what make the car run, but beyond that, you do not know what you are looking at.

If you were a camera, you would not even understand that much. It would be all totally meaningless.

The same is true of hearing. You might hear a strange noise and wonder what it is. You realize that it is a sound of some sort, but beyond that, what you are hearing is meaningless to you.

Similarly, you might overhear a conversation that does not make sense to you. You realize that you are listening to a foreign language, but beyond that, you do not know what is being said.

We could repeat this imaginative exercise with examples using the other senses: a smell that you cannot identify, a taste that is strange, an unexpected itch or pressure on the skin. But you get the point. Seeing, hearing, smelling, tasting and touching are sense experiences which, in themselves, are just that. They are just sensations unless they are also understood.

Usually we understand, at least vaguely, what our senses are sensing. But I have invited you to perform the little thought experiment to help you notice the difference between sensing and understanding.

If you were a robot, you could sense colors and sounds, for example, but you would not understand what you are seeing and hearing. (Let's not get into the notion of artificial intelligence or robots that might someday be able in the future to understand just as humans do. Talking about AI would take us off track.)

∗

Welcome to the world of meaning.

Everything that we "see" and "hear" above and beyond the raw data of colors and sounds is meaning of one sort or another.

The names of things are meanings. The uses of things are meanings. The benefits and dangers of things are meanings. This is the case not only with regard to what things are but also with regard to how they look. Colors, sizes and shapes are meaningful qualities. A camera could see them without understanding them. Every time we name, describe and discuss something we are talking about meanings. We understand what we are talking about because understandings and meanings are roughly the same.

Take a look at some of the things around you. See if you can discern the difference between the bare data that your eyes see and the meanings that your mind perceives.

Our understandings of sounds are meanings. If you hear someone speaking to you in English, what you pay attention to is the meaning of what is being said. The only time you pay attention to the sound is when the meaning is not coming through. For example, you might be listening to someone on a bad phone connection, and every now and then you fail to understand what is being said. At that point, you might say something like, "I can hear you talking but I cannot understand what you are saying." Your ear is picking up sounds but your mind is not perceiving any meaning.

Something similar happens when someone is singing and we cannot make out the words. We hear the sounds, but not the meaning.

The same is true when someone speaks to us in a foreign language. We hear the sounds they are making, but we are not able to understand what the person is trying to communicate. We don't get the meaning.

Language is not the only source of intelligible and unintelligible sounds. Walking in the woods, we can hear many sounds that we cannot identify. Someone who has learned to identify bird calls, however, can hear the same sound that we do and give it a name. In other words, birders can identify the sound and give it meaning. Likewise, we can be driving in our car and hear an unfamiliar noise. We don't know what it is, so we take the car to a mechanic who listens to the noise and tells us the car needs more power steering fluid.

Identify in your own experience times when you have heard sounds but did not know what they meant. Now reverse the thought experiment and remember a time when you explained the meaning of a sound to someone else, or interpreted a foreign language for someone.

*

Words have no meaning in themselves.

We usually assume that words have meanings, and that the meanings are in the words. This is because, when we read, the meanings of words and sentences come into our heads while we are looking at the physical words. Likewise, when we listen to something that is being said, the meanings of the words and sentences come into our heads while we are listening to the sounds.

The printed words or spoken words appear to be meaningful—or not, in the case when we do not understand what is written or spoken.

While you read these words on this page, the meanings of the words are occurring in your mind at the same time your eyes are looking at the words on the page. This simultaneity gives the impression that words have meanings, that words somehow contain meanings, and that the meanings are in the words.

However, we have already discussed how what the eye sees and what the mind understands are two different things. One is sensed and the other is understood. The same is true of what the ear hears and what the mind understands. One is a sound and the other is a meaning.

That words have no meaning in themselves is clear from the fact that we sometimes see words that we do not understand, and we sometimes hear words that we cannot interpret. That is, we have the appropriate visual or auditory sensations, but we do not know what they mean.

✶

Words are symbols.

A symbol refers to or points to something other than itself. The word "car," for example, refers to a machine on wheels in which you can travel. You can ride in a car, but you cannot ride in "car." That is, you can ride in what the word refers to, but you cannot ride in the word. The word symbolizes or refers to, in this case, a type of machinery.

Here is another example. My name is Joseph Martos. The name refers to someone who is a certain age, who can think and feel, and who can enter into relationships. The name, however, is not necessarily as old as I am, since my father had the same name. Moreover, the name cannot think or feel or enter into relationships. But I can. That is, what the name refers to can do those things, but the name cannot.

To make sure this idea is clear to you, come up with some of your own examples of things or people on the one hand, and the names that refer to them on the other hand.

The symbolic nature of words is easiest to illustrate with nouns that refer to concrete objects, but it also applies to verbs, adjectives and adverbs.

Growing is something that living things do, but the word itself does not grow. Any material object has weight, but the word "weight" does not weigh anything. A tall flagpole has a certain height, but the adjective "tall" cannot be measured. If I walk slowly, my walking speed can be measured, but the adverb "slowly" cannot.

If the difference between words and their referents (what they refer to) is not clear to you, try to make up some examples of your own.

✶

Symbols, like words, have no meaning in themselves.
We are used to thinking that symbols have meaning.

4

We travel to Europe and the road signs are different. We see signs like these:

We wonder what they mean, so we ask someone to explain the meaning to us. We get the feeling that the signs have meaning but we don't know what it is.

Looking at a road sign and not knowing what it means illustrates the fact that the meaning is not in the sign. Meanings are in human minds, not in symbols. But if we know what the road sign symbolizes, when we see the sign, we think the meaning.

Art, too, is sometimes symbolic. There is a famous painting by Jan Van Eyck of a man and woman being married.

Read an art history book about this painting and you will be told that it is full of symbolism. The woman's hand is in the man's, symbolizing that her life is in his hands. Both the bed and the woman's pregnancy symbolize fertility. The dog symbolizes fidelity, as does the man's hand raised as if taking an oath. The way they are dressed, the room's appointments and the oranges on the table (an exotic fruit in those days) are symbols of substantial but not excessive wealth.

If you were not told which elements of the painting are symbolic, and if you were not told the meaning of the symbols, their meaning would not be apparent. The meanings were in the mind of the artist, and then in the mind of the art historian, and finally in your mind when the painting is explained to you. But the meanings are not in the painting. Only oil paint is in the painting.

*

Some things are more important than others.

Thus far we have come to realize that much of what we take for granted in the world around us is meaningful. What we see and hear (and smell and touch and taste) are things that we understand to a greater or lesser extent. In fact, things that we don't understand are likely to be things that we don't even notice.

We can say, then, that anything that can be sensed (mainly physical or material realities) is sensible and also meaningful. Another way to say this is that such things are intelligible or able to be understood. "Intelligible" comes from the Latin word meaning to understand. The word "intellect" comes from the same Latin word.

At first, physical realities appear to be relatively simple. What's there to understand about a rock, a tree, or a bird? Upon further examination, however, physical realities can be very complex. Noticing and naming different types of rocks develops into the science of geology, and further examination can lead to understanding how different types of rocks came to be formed. Noticing and naming different types of plants develops into the science of biology, and the study of woody plants like trees is called dendrology. Noticing and naming animals is a different branch of biology, and the study of birds is ornithology.

Fields of study can divided and subdivided. One definition of a specialist is someone who knows more and more about less and less. Our point here, however, is that although the material world appears simple at first, investigation finds it to be exceedingly complex. At a certain point, eyes and ears no longer suffice to experience physical things, so microscopes and telescopes, microphones and recorders, and all sorts of imaging devices extend our eyes and ears beyond their natural limitations.

One might conclude that the material world encompasses all of reality from sub-atomic particles to entire galaxies, but the fact is there are realities that cannot be detected by our five senses or by any of the devices we use to extend them. How much does love weigh? How tall is justice? How wide is compassion? Such things cannot be measured in any usual sense. Yet they are real.

The fact that such things are elusive and hard to explain does not make them unreal. Something like justice might seem to be fairly abstract, but we all know when we are treating others fairly, and we all know how it feels to be cheated. We know intangible realities such as justice by intuition or feeling rather than by sensing. Non-material realities such as justice are hard to pin down. That's one reason why philosophers, essayists, novelists and poets are always writing about them.

Visitors to poor countries sometimes remark how happy the children are even though they do not have the toys and gadgets owned by most American children. The reason seems to be that they have caring parents and extended families within which they feel wanted and cherished. They have a sense of belonging, an awareness of community, and a sense of identity that comes in part from having responsibilities that contribute to the family's well-being. These are important but unmeasurable realities in the lives of such children.

We tend to overlook the importance of such realities by giving them names such as values or ideals or customs or mores. But these unmeasurable realities are the ones that make our lives human and happy. Family, friendship, acceptance, respect, purpose, responsibility, love, forgiveness, courage, fidelity, trust—such things are real but they are not measurable, and they are not material realities. In that very basic sense, they are spiritual realities.

Spiritual realities can be experienced, and they can be felt to be more or less intense, even if they cannot be measured. They can even be known to be absent. Someone who is lonely knows full well the absence of close relationships. Someone who has been cheated is quite aware that there is no justice in the current situation.

Take a minute to think about the immaterial realities that make your own life satisfying and make it meaningful. If you find it difficult to enumerate such things, ask yourself who or what would cause you the greatest grief if they were taken away. Chances are they won't be your house or car, but things that are real but not material.

*

Spiritual realities are meaningful.

Viktor Frankl was a Jewish prisoner in a Nazi concentration camp during World War II. As a young man living under such dehumanizing and stressful conditions, he noticed that some people were determined to survive, while others gave up and withered away. A psychologist by training, he wondered why some people lived and some died, even before being deported to one of the death camps. After the war, he reflected on his experiences and concluded that meaning and purpose made the difference. In one of the best-selling books of the 1960s, *Man's Search for Meaning*, Frankl wrote, "Those who have a 'why' to live, can bear with almost any 'how.'"

One's purpose in life is a spiritual reality. In a situation of total depravation, it can mean the difference between life and death. In a situation of relative affluence, having no purpose in life can lead to depression and despair, even suicide.

Whether it is a long-term goal or an immediate purpose, it is real, but it is not physical or material. It is a spiritual reality. Were it not real, it would have no effect on a real human being. Were it not real, its absence would make no difference to a person. To have an immediate purpose—to get through the day, to finish a task, to make enough to pay one's bills—can be motivation enough to get up in the morning and put up with all sorts of stress and drudgery.

When you have found it hard to make it through the day, was there a reason or purpose that kept you on task and helped you not to quit? If so, what was it?

Similarly, a long-term goal can provide the motivation to make it through a series of difficulties, whether anticipated or unanticipated, on the way to something that is valued or desired. We go to school in order to graduate, to find a job or enter a career that will enable us to provide for ourselves. We study a musical instrument, spending time developing our skill, for the gratification of accomplishment, and possibly for the entertainment and admiration of others. We do research, join a political movement or engage in social activism in order to make a difference in the world or to make people's lives better. Such a vision of the future, no matter how vague, gives our life direction and gives it a meaning that it would not otherwise have.

If you were to ask what gives meaning to your life, how would you answer? Are you someone who is goal-oriented in the sense that there is something you would like to accomplish before you die? If so, what is that goal? Apart from that, what gives your life meaning? What do you hope people say about you when they talk about you?

We have moved well beyond the meaning of physical objects and material things. When we begin to think about these larger issues, we enter the realm of what makes us human, and what makes life worth living. We are into the realm of relationships and commitments, values and ideals, purposes and principles that rocks and trees do not have, and that lizards and birds cannot begin to imagine. We are into the realm of spirit.

*

Language communicates ideas and other spiritual realities.

We live in a world where communication is so plentiful that we fail to notice it. We don't know who discovered water, but we are pretty sure it wasn't a fish. Fish are surrounded by water. It is in fact the environment in which they live, so they notice things in their watery environment but they do not notice the water itself.

In the same way, we do not notice the communications environment in which we live when we use elements in that environment to communicate with one another. Whether we use email or old-fashioned letters, whether we use Facebook or Instagram, whether we use texting or Twitter or whatever the next technology will be, our focus is on the message and not on the medium. We are thinking about what we are trying to get across, not about the technology we are using.

A fundamental communication technology is language. Most languages, like English, try to capture sounds in such a way that, if you know the alphabet, you can say the sounds even if you do not understand what the words mean. This aspect of our communication technology is normally invisible to us, but it becomes more visible if we consider words that are written in other alphabets, such as these:

Greek	εξουσία, πίστη, αεροπλάνο
Russian	отправился, новый, город
Hebrew	בֶּן אָדָם, עֵמֶק, בֵּית מִקְדָּשׁ
Arabic	صحراء, اعمال, القرآن الكريم

There are also written languages such as Chinese and Japanese that do not enable the reader to say the sounds that it represents. Such languages use ideograms to symbolize ideas directly. Ideograms were originally developed in the Far East so that people who spoke different dialects could communicate with one another. Looking at the ideogram, two individuals could get the same idea, even if they had different spoken words for that idea. In Chinese, for example, these ideograms would be spoken differently in Mandarin or Cantonese:

請 在 上 海 找 個 家

It is relatively easy to preserve and communicate ideas in written languages. But how did human beings preserve and communicate ideas before writing was invented about five thousand years ago? They told stories and repeated actions.

✳

Ideas and values need to be remembered and communicated.

Myth and ritual have gotten a bad reputation in our day. When someone wants to dismiss a story as worthless, they might say, "That's just a myth." And when someone wants to denigrate religion, they might say, "It's all a bunch of ritual." We have come a long way from the original purpose of myths and rituals in pre-literate societies, that is, in societies that existed before the invention of writing.

Myth and ritual are the information storage and retrieval system of pre-literate societies. Myths are stories that preserve and communicate ideas in the form of a narrative. The two biblical creation myths are a good example of this. The first tells a story of the world being created in six days and God resting on the seventh. The second tells a story of God creating the first man, then making the barren world flourish with plant and animal life, and finally creating the first woman.

For centuries, Christians took the stories literally (and some still do), but scholars who study myth tell us that we should ignore the details and think of the big picture. The first story told listeners (long before the stories were edited and written down) that there is a higher power in the universe, that it is important to rest from work regularly, that the natural world is good, and that men and women are created in the image of God. Incidentally, the story is also a rudimentary lesson in astronomy, meteorology and biology, for it captures what human beings understood about their physical environment at the time: the stars are up, rain comes down, and the world is full of things that are good to eat. The second story communicates many of the same understandings, plus the fact that the sexes find fulfillment in each other, that the evil in the world is not God's fault, that blaming is a way of denying responsibility, and that life is hard.

Even today, storytellers realize that a good story is built around an idea or a string of ideas that are tied together in a narrative. If you have ever told bedtime stories to your children (Think of Goldilocks or the Three Little Pigs.), you know this to be the case. There may be some events that need to be told in sequence, and there may be some sentences that are memorably repeatable ("Who's been sleeping in MY bed?" or "I'll huff and I'll puff and I'll blow your house down!"), but the words are not like a script in a play that have to be mechanically repeated time after time. If you tell ghost stories around a campfire, or cowboy tales, or Native American legends, you tell the same story every time even if you never tell the story exactly the same way twice. There is no such thing as literalism in an oral culture. The ideas are important, not the words.

In many tribal cultures, a story is true if it describes the way people ought to behave, and it is false if it fails to do so. In such "true" stories, values and morals are preserved and passed from one generation to the next, whether or not the events they describe ever actually happened. *The Iliad* and *The Odyssey* preserved the values and virtues of Greek warrior culture: tales told by men to other men about how to be real men.

Examples of rituals that preserve and pass along information are harder to identify in our culture. So many of the items we use are pre-fabricated, and we have no sense of the sequence of steps that needed to be performed, repeated, and passed from one generation to the next if people were to have cloth, shoes, or candles, not to mention food that had to be grown from year to year.

In early tribal societies, huts were often built according to the specifications contained in myths, and canoes were dug out from tree trunks in a ritual fashion that ensured their seaworthiness. When Samurai swords were made by hand, every step of the process was strictly regulated by time-honored rituals. Boys learned hunting motions in dances before they ever joined a hunt with the men in their tribe. Girls learned how the ancients taught the first humans what is edible before they were allowed to forage for their family.

If you have ever spun wool, or woven cloth, or made an article of clothing, you have a sense of how important ritual is for doing things repeatedly and successfully. If you have ever made a broom from straw, or made a rope from hemp, or built a shed from raw lumber, you have a sense of how important ritual is for learning how to do things right.

*

Meaning points to what is meant.

Even though we assume that symbols have meaning in the sense that the meaning is somehow in the symbols, our analysis has shown that meaning is in human minds and not in the ink and paper, or paint and canvas, or stone, or metal out of which symbols are made.

What is the source of this assumption? Why do we believe that there is meaning in symbols?

Part of the reason is that words and symbols are in the world around us. We hear them with our ears and we see them with our eyes. If we are in a healthy and waking state of mind, we can tell the difference between what is perceived in our environment and what is generated by our own mind. If we are dreaming, we cannot tell the difference, but when we wake up, we can. If we are experiencing hallucinations or suffering from delusions, we may not be able to tell the difference, but those are not normal states of mind.

Ordinarily we look at objects with our eyes, and we hear sounds with our ears. When the objects we look at are meaningful to us—or to say it another way, when they are intelligible to us—we understand what we are looking at. Likewise, when the sounds we hear are meaningful to us, we understand what we are hearing.

Our analysis has shown that the visible aspect of things we look at comes from the outside, as it were. We have a sense, and correctly so, that physical objects are outside us. At the same time, however, the meaning or intelligibility that we ascribe to those objects occurs within us. It is in our mind. Since the meaning is not literally in the objects, it must be something that is added by our mind to what we see with our eyes.

It is a little like ascribing human thoughts to our household pets. Dogs and cats don't think the way we do, but we interpret their behavior as though they did think when they behave in ways that people might. I have a friend who believes that his dog is asking to go out in the back yard to relieve herself whenever she stands by the back door. Since he gives her a treat whenever she comes back in the house, I think she has been conditioned to stand by the door because she is rewarded for going out and coming back in—whether or not she has done any business in the yard.

In the same way, but much more frequently, we look at things around us, like the coffee cup on my desk, and my mind spontaneously combines the visual image of the cup with the understanding of what it is into a perception of something that has meaning for me.

So it is that when we look at symbols or hear words, our mind spontaneously combines the sense data with an idea, resulting in the perception of a meaningful object or a meaningful utterance. Since we can look at things that are meaningful to others but not to ourselves, and since we can hear things that are meaningful to others but not to ourselves, we have to conclude that meaning is not "out there" but in our conscious mind.

At the same time, we have to recognize that the meaningful objects in our field of vision and the meaningful sounds that we hear are perceived as being "out there" in the world. When we talk about a flower, for example, what is meant is the flower that we are looking at. And when we talk about a promise, what is meant is a promise that has been made by someone.

We may find it easy to talk about meaning, for we use that word often. We talk about the meaning of words, the meaning of symbols, the meaning of a poem, the meaning of a gesture, and so on. But we do not often use the word "meant" unless there is some uncertainty about what is being referred to. We might ask, for example, what was meant by some statement or what was meant by some gesture?

To avoid confusion, therefore, we shall use the word "referent" when discussing what words and symbols refer to. The referent is what is meant when we talk about something meaningful in the world around us. It is also what is meant when we talk about something meaningful that we experience, like joy or sorrow, courage or fear, love or hate.

Such emotions are spiritual realities in the sense already discussed. They cannot be weighed or measured, and so they are not physical or material realities. But they are no less real.

✳

Spiritual realities are not seen or heard, but they are felt and understood.

We tend to think of joy and sorrow, courage and fear, love and hate as feelings. There is no denying that they are. But they are also feelings through which spiritual realities are perceived.

Just as colors are sense data through which we perceive things in the world around us, and just as sounds are sense data through which we perceive what is being said to us, so also feelings are internal data through which we perceive things that are invisible but no less real.

If love were only a feeling, then there would be no such thing as real love. We could not look at a couple hugging each other and say they love each other. We could only say that they have feelings of love. We could not hear about a mother waking in the middle of the night to respond to a crying infant and say that she loves her baby. We could see a daughter staying in a hospital at her dying father's bedside, but we could not say she loves her dad. We could not see a young man marching off to war and say he loves his country. We could only say that those people have loving feelings of some sort. But that's not what we say. Through their behavior, we perceive that they are motivated by love, even if they are not feeling love all the time.

We know what love feels like, and we know how we behave when we love someone or something, so when we see someone behaving that way, we perceive their love. We cannot get inside their minds, and we cannot feel their feelings, but we can understand that they are acting out of love. Certainly we can be deceived, just as we can be deceived by an optical illusion or by a lie, but in most cases we can say that we know real love when we see it.

The same is true of hate. If hate were only a feeling, there would be no such thing as real hate. If a man committed a hate crime but showed no signs of hatred or anger when he was caught, could he be arrested if he was no longer feeling hate?

From examples like these, we can infer that spiritual realities are not just feelings. They can also be values or habits or principles or motivations. Someone who commits a hate crime may not always be feeling hatred, but his hate might motivate him to do something to damage property or hurt people.

At the beginning of this section, I also mentioned joy and sorrow, courage and fear as spiritual realities. Fear can be a very strong feeling, but it can also be a motivation to lock doors, to avoid certain neighborhoods, or to carry a weapon even when we are not feeling frightened. Courage is hardly ever a feeling; it is more often a habit or a principle of action in situations that call for it. Joy and sorrow are certainly felt realities, and they can also motivate people to behave differently than they ordinarily do.

Is this argument making sense to you? Can you agree that some of the things you feel are more than just feelings? If so, can you come up with your own examples of things that you feel that are more than just feelings?

✳

We have been building our case for spiritual realities slowly.

We started off talking about material things, pointing out that we know them not just through our senses but also with our minds. What we understand about things is not found in any of their physical properties, but in our mind. In a sense, there is a spiritual dimension even to material objects: their intelligibility is something that our mind understands and not something that our eyes see.

Talking about words and symbols was the next step. We take for granted that words and symbols have meaning, but we have seen that written or spoken signs are things that we understand when we experience them. That we can also experience them without understanding them shows that the understanding or meaning is not in words and symbols but in our mind.

Next, we talked about spiritual realities that are known through feelings. At this point, we got into things like love and courage and joy that are not as definite as material objects or physical sounds. But they are experienced, and this is important. We know love when we have experienced it, either as a feeling in ourselves or as a behavior we have seen in others. We know courage when we muster our determination to do something that is dangerous, and also when we see someone acting with determination in a dangerous situation. We know joy when we experience it ourselves, and also when we recognize it in the faces of others.

Is it possible that there are spiritual realities that go beyond the ones we have talked about? Are there things that cannot be experienced directly but are nonetheless real? There are, and we are now in a position to talk about them.

✳

Social realities are spiritual realities.

Is society real? What about the economy? And what about government? Are neighborhoods and towns and cities and counties and states and countries real? Or are they figments of our imagination, convenient fictions that human beings invent to impose some order on people living together?

For that matter, what about law? What about justice and injustice? What about morality and ethics? Are huge things like this, things that transcend individual people, real or not?

Philosophical materialists, individualists and libertarians would say not. Margaret Thatcher, the prime minister of Great Britain in the 1980s, once said, "There is no such thing as society: there are individual men and women, and there are families."

But what is a family if not a collection of relationships? People may be related by blood, or as we say today, genetically, but does that make them a family? If a father disowns his children, are they still family? If a girl runs away from home and never sees her parents again, does she have a family any more? If an unmarried couple adopts children, can they be a family? And what of an extended family that includes individuals who are genetically related and others who are not?

If Thatcher had been a consistent individualist, she would have said, "There are only individuals: there is no such thing as family, society or any other collection of people. Such collections are convenient fictions created to organize individuals." Margaret Thatcher spontaneously assumed that families are real, despite her philosophy of rugged individualism.

Proving the actual existence of social realities is philosophically difficult, and not something to be attempted in a book such as this one. Suffice it to say that ordinary people assume that relationships and values and principles are real, even though they are hard to pin down and define.

We shall assume they are real, as well. Personally, I think it's a safe bet.

Put it this way. If relationships and values and principles are not real, then there is no such thing as a real friendship, there is no such thing as genuine goodness, and there is no such thing as actual justice. Most of us would not want to live in a world like that.

*

Some spiritual realities are more important than others.

Remember what I said about the fish and water? We don't ordinarily notice our environment; it surrounds us and makes our world be what it is. It's like air: we don't notice it when it's there, but if we can't inhale, we suddenly notice that something is missing

Most of us live in a web of relationships. We relate to members of our family, we have classmates at school and acquaintances at work, we join hobby clubs or sports associations, we belong to a church, we are active in a political party, and so on. Imagine how life would be without any social network at all. Imagine being in solitary confinement. Or imagine being in a big city without knowing anyone.

From such an imaginative perspective, it is easy to see the importance of acceptance and belonging. Or maybe there were times in your life when you felt really alone, with no one to trust and no one to talk to. Or maybe you did not feel particularly lonely, but then you met someone you could really connect with, someone who seemed to understand you, someone with whom you could freely share your thoughts and feelings. A connection was made, a bond was established.

From imaginative examples like these, or from examples in your own life, you can appreciate the value of community. It can be a community of two, like a partnership or marriage. It can be a community of a few, or even a small bunch, like the people on a sports team or a theater group. It can be a community of relatives, like a family.

Such relationships are often celebrated, for example, by going out on a date, by having a meal together, by having a party, or by going out to a bar together. It's just fun to feel those relationships when we are in one another's company.

Moreover, what we do often symbolizes those relationships, albeit in unconscious and culturally determined ways. We shake hands, we hug, we kiss. We say what's going on in our lives, we share ideas and opinions, we talk about our feelings, and when we do this, we are putting into symbolic form—words, gestures, facial expressions, and body movements—what we think, what we feel, and, to a greater or lesser extent, who we are. The longer and deeper such exchanges go, the stronger the relationships become. At the end, we say good-bye, we hug or kiss again, and we end our time together with the same sort of culturally appropriate rituals with which the celebration began.

Acceptance, belonging, trust, forgiveness, honesty, openness, generosity, faithfulness—spiritual realities such as these are pretty important in our lives as human beings. Other things such as power or fame or wealth or pleasure can seem very important at times, but without spiritual realities such as love, fidelity and community, it is hard to enjoy them for very long. Novels and autobiographies are filled with stories of people who got everything they thought they wanted but still felt empty and unfulfilled.

2

Metaphors and Metaphysics

MANY OF THE WORDS we use are metaphors.

Twelve inches make a foot, but this measurement of length derives from the average length of an adult foot. Teeth are found in humans and other animals, but someone decided long ago that they are also found in combs. Stretch the meaning of the word a little more, and it could mean enforceability, as in a law that has teeth. We can pile boxes in a stack, but we can also have a stack of work to do, and things can get stacked against us.

Metaphors come into language when someone wants to express a meaning for which there is no word. In this case, an older word gets put to new use. Glass was originally a translucent substance made from melted sand, and when drinking vessels were made from it, they got called glasses. When it became possible to improve vision using glass that was shaped and polished, the new inventions were also called glasses.

Inventors often coin new words to name their inventions. The telegraph was named from two Greek words meaning distance and write; likewise the telephone from the Greek for distance and speak. The car was first called a horseless carriage, but when they stopped looking like wagons with engines, they were called automobiles from Greek words meaning self and moving. Words coined from other languages are also metaphors of sorts.

Once we become used to the different meanings of words, we can still tell what a word with multiple possible meanings refers to. Depending on the context of the discussion, for example, we can determine whether a particular sentence is about glasses that we use for drinking or glasses that we wear in order to see better.

This is another indication that meanings are in minds and not in words or even in sense data. Depending on what is meant, the meaning in the mind is different. Since the same word can have two or more referents, the meaning cannot be in the word. And since meaning is not something that is seen by the eyes, heard by the ears, or sensed in any other way, it must be an understanding that is in the mind.

*

Languages grow by using metaphors and by inventing new words.

No one was around to record the origin of human language, nor for that matter, the origins of the many human languages. We can imagine, however, that ancient languages grew the same way that contemporary language grows, that is, by giving old words new meanings and by inventing new ones. We give old words new meanings by using them to refer to new things, by giving them new referents. When I was young, for example, being gay meant being happy, but today being gay means being homosexual. Similarly, being straight meant the opposite of being crooked or dishonest, but today being straight means being heterosexual. When the referents of words change, their meanings change.

New words recently added to the English language include selfie, texting, and sexting. These words refer to things that could not be done before the invention of smart phones. Notice how the new words are metaphors in the sense that they take an old word and change it slightly in order to refer to something new.

English is full of words and phrases that have become so common that we no longer recognize them as metaphors. We talk about the sun rising and setting, for example, even though we no longer think of the earth as stationary and the sun moving around it. Can you think of other words or figures of speech that were probably once metaphors but today are used without thinking of their original referent? (Hint: Name calling and other forms of foul language are a good source here.)

New words are being added to the English language all the time. The same was true of ancient languages even though the process of language growth was much slower then.

★

The Bible contains some ancient metaphors.

Among the best known is the Hebrew word, *meshiach*. (Note that this is a transliteration of מָשִׁיחַ, which you probably cannot read. A transliteration tells you how a foreign word is pronounced. It is different from a translation, which tells you what a foreign word means.) This is the word from which we get the English word, "messiah." Actually, "messiah" is also a transliteration of the Hebrew word, although it is not as close to the original pronunciation.

Christians are familiar with the idea that the Jews in ancient times were hoping for a *meshiach* or messiah that would save them from the Roman Empire, under whose rule they had been living since 63 BC. What was so special about a messiah that the Jews thought that he (There were no female messiahs back then.) could defeat the Romans?

You may be aware that *meshiach* means anointed. The Old Testament speaks about prophets being anointed and kings being anointed. This did not necessarily mean that prophets and kings had oil poured over their heads—although sometime they were physically anointed as a sign that they were inwardly anointed.

What did it mean, then, to say that a prophet or king was anointed? And what did it mean to say that a hoped-for military leader would be anointed? In other words, what did the word refer to? If it did not refer to someone with oily hair, the word *meshiach* must be a metaphor.

To what, then, did the metaphor point? What was it trying to name by using the word *meshiach* to talk about people who had not been physically anointed, as Jewish priests were when they were appointed to perform their service in the Temple.

Think about it. What did prophets and kings have in common? What did they have that ordinary people did not have? Jewish prophets were God's spokespersons. They told the people what God wanted the people to hear. In other words, they had an ability to do something that ordinary people did not have. Jewish kings, at least at the beginning, were not part of a royal family. They were chosen because they had leadership abilities on and off the battlefield.

We would say they were gifted. They had abilities or talents that other people did not have. And this is why the Jews in Jesus' time were waiting for a *meshiach*. They were waiting for someone who could do what they themselves could not do.

Notice that "gifted" is also a metaphor. To call someone gifted does not literally mean that they have received more presents than someone else. Calling someone gifted entails stretching the meaning of the word "gift" so that it means an extraordinary ability or an unusual talent.

We say that someone is gifted. The people of Israel said that someone is anointed. Both words have the same referent. They both refer to abilities that are unusual and in some way special.

⋆

The New Testament continued the Old Testament practice.

We have seen that Jews in the first century were hoping for a messiah, or someone with the ability to free Israel from the oppressive rule of the Roman Empire.

Jesus was also called a messiah, and now we know why. He was a person with abilities that ordinary people do not have. He was a gifted speaker. He had the ability to heal people's physical and spiritual ailments. He had a talent for debating with the religious leaders of his day.

He was a messiah, even if he was not the kind of messiah that most people were looking for.

In Hebrew, he would have been called *meshiach*. The New Testament was written in Greek, however, and its authors chose to translate that word into Greek rather than to transliterate it. The word they chose was the Greek word for someone who is anointed. The word is *christos*. (Note that this is a transliteration of the Greek word, χρίστος, which you cannot read unless you are familiar with the Greek alphabet. So the Greeks translated *meshiach* into *christos*, but we transliterate *christos* into christ. Greek at the time did not capitalize proper nouns, but English does, and so *christos* most often becomes Christ in translations of the New Testament.)

The word *christos* literally means oiled or anointed. In the sacrament of confirmation, Catholics use a scented oil called chrism, in Greek, *chrisma*.

In older translations of the Bible, the Greek word *christos* was almost always rendered as Christ. In Matthew 16, Jesus asks his disciples, "Who do people say that I am?" In the King James Bible, Peter's answer is, "Thou art the Christ." In the New American Bible, his answer is, "You are the messiah." A translation that reflected the Hebrew usage might be, "You are the anointed one."

A translation based on what has been said here might be, "You are the gifted one."

How might this affect your understanding of Jesus as messiah or Christ?

*

There are other metaphors in the New Testament.

In chapter 12 of the First Letter to the Corinthians, Paul is speaking to a community of converts who were pagans before he brought the message of Christ to them. Some of them apparently did not "get the message" because they were being selfish instead of compassionate, and they were arguing over who was the best among them. In setting the record straight, Paul uses a number of metaphors.

In the very first verse, Paul announces that he is going to talk about spiritual matters (*pneumatika*), but by "spiritual" Paul has in mind things that can be experienced. He refers to them as gifts (*charismata*) not in the sense of material presents but in the sense of things that have been received from God. Some members of the community are able to pray in strange languages (sometimes called speaking in tongues), others have the ability to translate those prayers, still others are able to say what God wants the community to hear, and there are some who are able to heal people the way Jesus did. By using the metaphor of "gift," Paul is interpreting the various abilities as being given by a single spiritual source, namely God.

Insisting that no spiritual gift is better than others, Paul invokes another metaphor—a living human body. Not only are they a community of believers, he argues, but they are members of the body of Christ, with each part making a valuable contribution to the whole (1 Corinthians 12:12–31).

It is important to notice here that Paul is using this metaphor in order to teach a lesson about group cohesion and cooperation to a distinct group of people living in Corinth during the first decades of Christianity. Undoubtedly it is a lesson that other communities, Christian and otherwise, can benefit from. In time, however, Christian thinkers turned the metaphor into a metaphysical reality, that is, they claimed that the entire church (not just an individual community) was the body of Christ even if it contained thousands or millions of people.

It's a long way from metaphor to metaphysics, but it is a path that has been frequently traveled by Christian intellectuals through the centuries.

*

Baptism is a prime source of metaphors in the New Testament.

Various theories have been proposed to explain why baptism became such an important practice in the early church. Jesus' cousin John baptized people who were interested in moral regeneration, or to put it in the language of the times, in repenting of their sins. But there is no evidence that the people baptized by John formed themselves into communities for mutual moral support.

Jews for some time had practiced a form of ritual immersion for pagans who wanted to convert to the faith of Abraham and Moses, and who wanted to adopt the Jewish way of life. Proselyte baptism, as it was called, ritually symbolized the passing of the Israelites through the Jordan River in order to enter the Promised Land. Since the earliest followers of Jesus thought of themselves as Jews who had accepted the teachings of the anointed one, it seems reasonable to suppose that when non-Jews wanted to join their community, they would have been initiated through this ritual practice.

By the mid-fist century, when Paul of Tarsus was actively engaging in missionary work, some of the converts displayed behaviors similar to those found in charismatic prayer groups and Pentecostal churches today—praying in tongues, prophesying aloud, and healing through the laying-on of hands, for example. Such manifestations of religious fervor have been found in other religions, so it is possible that when Christians began exhibiting them, there was a vocabulary at hand with which to name them such as glossolalia, prophesying and healing.

When Paul tried to talk about other, less noticeable, aspects of conversion and community, however, he had to resort to metaphors. We have already seen him using the metaphor of the body.

In his letter to the community in Rome, which he had not yet visited, he wrote

> Do you not know that we who were baptized into Christ Jesus were baptized into his death? We were therefore buried with him through baptism into death, so that just as Christ was raised from

the dead by the glory of the Father, we too might live a new life.
(Romans 6:3–4)

First, we ought to ask how Paul could say this about baptism? Either he was making it up, or he was inspired by God to say it, or he was saying something based on his own experience. We should presume that Paul was being honest and knew what he was talking about. Also, the inspiration theory does not contribute much if Paul did not know what he was saying. So let us assume that he was talking out of his experience.

Next, we ought to be aware that "baptize" is a transliteration of the Greek word *baptizō*; it is not a translation. If the word were translated, it would be "immerse." And we can translate the Greek word *eis* as "in" rather than as "into" because in English we talk about being immersed in something, not immersed into something.

Retranslating the passage using these substitutions, it becomes

> Do you not know that we who were immersed in Christ Jesus were immersed in his death? We were therefore buried with him in death through immersion, so that just as Christ was raised from the dead by the glory of the Father, we too might live a new life. (Romans 6:3–4)

Notice the low christology here. Christ is not equated with God, but he is raised from the dead by the power of God. More about high and low christology later.

Next, I would suggest that, for Paul, the phrase "Christ Jesus" is a metaphor for the Christian community, which Paul regarded as the body of Christ animated by his spirit. (See also Romans 6:11, 6:23, 8:1–2, 8:39.) As he wrote to the Corinthians, "We were all immersed in one spirit and formed into one body" (1 Corinthians 12:13). Elsewhere, the phrase *en christo* also seems to be a metaphor meaning in the body of Christ, or in the Christian community. (Romans 12:5, 16:3, 16:7, 16:9; 1 Corinthians 1:4, 1:30, 4:15, 15:18, 15:22, 15:31, 16:24). Paul seems to be saying that life in Christ, which is life in the Christian community, is different from life outside the community. Anyone who has been a member of an intentional religious community such as a charismatic prayer group knows what Paul is talking about.

In the passage above, from Romans 6, Paul claims that those who are immersed in the Christian community are immersed in his death. Again we must ask what Paul is talking about, especially if what he is saying is based on his own experience. Further in the same letter, he speaks about being "dead to sin but alive to God in Christ Jesus" (6:11). Is it not plausible that Paul is speaking here about moral conversion—his own and others that he has witnessed in Christian communities? In the experience of such conversion, people metaphorically die to a way of life that is full of moral shortcomings (The Greek word for sin, *hamartia*, means literally falling short or missing the mark.) and they are metaphorically reborn to a new life, that is, a new lifestyle that is supported by a community of believers. In other words, just as Jesus died in order to do God's will and was raised by God to new life, so also those who die to their sinful ways in order to do God's will experience personal regeneration in a body that has been raised to new life. The parallel between Christ's death and resurrection and the convert's death to sin and new life in a supportive community is, in Paul's mind, close enough that one can be used as a metaphor for the other.

Later in the history of Christianity, however, Paul's words were taken not as a metaphor for moral conversion and a new way of life but as a metaphysical transformation that results from ritual participation in a baptism ceremony.

To illustrate what I am talking about, here are some excerpts from the Catholic Rite of Baptism for Children.

> By the mystery of your death and resurrection, bathe this child in light, give him (her) the new life of baptism and welcome him (her) into your holy Church.

- This asks Christ to miraculously bestow the benefits of his death and resurrection on the child by giving it new spiritual life.

> Through baptism and confirmation, make him (her) your faithful follower and a witness to your gospel.

- This asks Christ to make the child a faithful follower and witness to the gospel without the child having to do anything.

> We pray for this child: set him (her) free from original sin, make him (her) a temple of your glory, and send your Holy Spirit to dwell with him (her).

- This asks God to free the child from a sin it has not committed, to make the child a temple God's glory, and to send the Holy Spirit into the child, without the child being aware of any of this.

> We anoint you with the oil of salvation in the name of Christ our Savior; may he strengthen you with his power, who lives and reigns for ever and ever.

- This asks God to bestow moral and religious strength through the ritual application of oil.

> We ask you, Father, with your Son to send the Holy Spirit upon the water of this font. May all who are buried with Christ in the death of baptism rise also with him to newness of life.

- This asks God to send the Holy Spirit on the baptismal water, in the expectation that the ritual will automatically bring about dying to sin and rising to new life.

> I baptize you in the name of the Father, and of the Son, and of the Holy Spirit.

- Note that the child need not do anything in order to be baptized and receive its spiritual benefits.

> God the Father of our Lord Jesus Christ has freed you from sin, given you a new birth by water and the Holy Spirit, and welcomed you into his holy people.

- This announces that God has done everything through the performance of the ritual.

> You have become a new creation, and have clothed yourself in Christ.

- Again, this announces a *fait accompli*.

> You have put on Christ, in him you have been baptized.

- This says that the child has done something when in fact it has done nothing, and it suggests that baptism into Christ is automatic.

Clearly, the words of the rite suggest that something is going on behind the scene while the ceremony is being performed. In terms of our discussion until now, what is believed to be going on is unseen, it is literally meta-physical, beyond the realm of the physical world.

Moreover, because the invisible effects of the rite are said to be brought about by the performance of certain actions in the visible world, a rite such as this can be said to be an exercise in ritual magic. It is action at a distance, the production of spiritual effects by doing certain things in the material world.

This metaphysical interpretation of baptism is a far cry from the metaphorical interpretation discussed above, and also from the metaphor in the letter to the Galatians, where Paul says, "You who have been baptized into Christ have put on Christ" (3:27), which is very likely a metaphorical way of saying, "You who have been immersed in the Christian community have assumed a Christian identity." He is saying something analogous to "You're in the army now, so now you are soldiers."

My point is that Paul is talking to adults who have decided to throw their lot in with the Christians and who are now expected to follow the teachings of Jesus. He is not suggesting anything metaphysical or magical, the way the Catholic rite of baptism does.

✳

Words used in the rite of confirmation reveal a similar mentality.

The Catholic sacrament of confirmation is a historical accident that was given a metaphysical interpretation in the Middle Ages.

During the first three centuries of Christianity, converts were initiated into the Christian community through a lengthy process (up to three years) of moral conversion that culminated in a ritual celebration of the conversion process. The performance of a ceremonial immersion ritualized the changes that had been going on in the initiate's life during long the period of instruction and probation. The surviving documents of that period such as the *Didachē* (the abbreviated Greek title of a work called *The Teaching of the Twelve Apostles* but not actually written by any of them) talks about the Christian way of life but does not have much to say about what was later known as Christian doctrine, namely beliefs about God, Christ, the Holy Spirit, and the church.

Looking back on the conversion process, initiates could see that they had died to their old way of life, that they had become immersed in a new community and a new lifestyle, and that they were now different from what they were before. The first part of the ritual celebration involved being partly or fully immersed in water. The second part was either being anointed with oil or receiving a laying on of hands (or both) symbolizing that they had received the gift of the Spirit of God from above. The third part was sharing a special meal for the first time with the rest of the community they were joining.

Since the ceremony required initiates to go into the baptismal water completely divested of all clothing and jewelry (symbolic of having died to their previous life), deacons attended to the immersion of men and deaconesses attended to the immersion of women. After their immersion and the recital of ritual vows, they were given a new white garment to wear, symbolizing the new life into which they had entered. They then went before the supervisor or bishop of the community, who anointed them or laid hands on them. Finally, they shared what Paul had called the Lord's Supper, which until then they had been forbidden to participate in.

When communities were relatively small, the bishop of the community could preside over the second part to bless and receive each of the initiates. In the fourth century, however, communities grew too large for a single annual ceremony. Local parishes were established and multiple initiation ceremonies were held in each city at Easter or Pentecost. The bishop could not be present to bless and receive all of the new Christians, so changes were introduced. In the East, the bishop's presence was symbolized by using oil that he had blessed beforehand. In the West, initiates were asked to present themselves to the bishop at a later date to receive the anointing or laying on of hands. Thus the bishop's part in the initiation ritual got separated from the immersion, not intentionally but by force of circumstances.

In the Christian West, which is to say the European churches that used Latin as their liturgical language, the confirmation of baptisms declined after the fall of the Roman Empire. Cities shrank and the population became more rural. Roads were almost nonexistent and travel became more difficult. Some bishops used creative theologizing to persuade parents to bring their children for confirmation, promising that the sacrament would be spiritually strengthening, but their efforts were for the most part ineffective.

Charlemagne's Holy Roman Empire brought a modicum of stability to the western part of Europe in the ninth century, and some well-intentioned bishops tried to revitalize the sacrament. They attributed excerpts from episcopal sermons to early popes and promulgated them as official church doctrine, but even this attempt at reform did not last. During most of the Middle Ages, it was mainly the clergy who were given the sacrament of confirmation since it was a pre-requisite for being ordained. This cultural fact was reflected in the sacramental theology of Thomas Aquinas and other schoolmen who concluded that confirmation bestowed a certain strengthening of the faith, sometimes citing the example of the Holy Spirit descending on the apostles at Pentecost.

From then until now, the sacramental rite has remained an example of metaphysical thinking, for it purports to bestow spiritual benefits on those who are confirmed even though it has no apparent effects on them. The disconnect between the rite and reality is illustrated by the variety of policies around the United States regulating confirmation. In some dioceses, teenagers are confirmed before graduating from high school, in others youngsters are confirmed before graduating from elementary school, and in still others children are confirmed before first communion, usually in the second grade. The debate about the proper age for confirmation continues because the sacrament has no necessary connection to Catholics at any point in their lives.

The rite of confirmation is short. Here are some excerpts.

> Let us pray to our Father that he will pour out the Holy Spirit to strengthen his sons and daughters with his gifts and anoint them to be more like Christ the Son of God.

- The usual minister of the sacrament is the bishop. Here he prays that God will do something for them that is beyond their awareness.

> All-powerful God, Father of our Lord Jesus Christ, by water and the Holy Spirit you freed your sons and daughters from sin and gave them new life. Send your Holy Spirit upon them to be their Helper and Guide. Give them the spirit of wisdom and understanding, the spirit of right judgment and courage, the spirit of knowledge and reverence. Fill them with the spirit of wonder and awe in your presence.

- His prayer continues in the same vein, asking for the bestowal of spiritual gifts that can be prayed for by anyone at any time. The first sentence of this prayer makes reference to the supposed metaphysical effects of baptism.

> Be sealed with the Gift of the Holy Spirit.

- It is difficult to explain what these words refer to. How is one sealed with a gift, or sealed with a spirit?

Pronounced solemnly and officiously, the words of the sacramental rite can seem to be very important—until one looks at them closely.

✶

What good is an invisible sign?

Catholics are asked to believe that some sacraments bestow an indelible seal, also called a sacramental character or an invisible sign of belonging to Christ. Found in the theology of baptism and confirmation, it is an excellent example of how a biblical metaphor got turned into a metaphysical entity.

Four places in the New Testament talk about a seal or being sealed. In the Second Letter to the Corinthians, Paul writes,

> God who binds us and you together in the anointed one, has anointed us, put a seal on us, and sent his spirit into our hearts as a pledge of more to come. (2 Corinthians 1:21–22)

One of the first questions we have to ask is: How did Paul know this? Where did he get his information?

Too often Christians read the Bible assuming that the author was inspired to write what he did, and so the job of the interpreter is to figure out what he meant. Very often this is done by looking at how a word is used in context and comparing it to other places where the word is used. While that might be a good procedure in some cases, in Paul's case it is very likely that he was drawing many of his ideas from his own experience when he expressed ideas that cannot be found elsewhere. I have already argued this point with regard to baptism.

What then may have led Paul to write these words to the community in Corinth? What was he talking about?

We have already seen that when Paul speaks about being united in Christ, or the anointed one, he is talking about being together in the body of Christ, the Christian community. Just as Jesus was anointed or gifted, Paul is saying that Christians have been given a variety of spiritual gifts, as talked about in the previous letter he wrote to the Corinthians. Such external manifestations are an outward sign or a visible seal indicating what lies within, namely God's spirit. Paul assures his readers that this experience is a promise of more to come.

The word "seal" in this passage (*sphragis*) is an outward sign of something that is within, the way that a seal imposed on a letter in the ancient world was an indication of what the letter might contain.

Let us now follow the more usual path and compare Paul's use of *sphragis* here with other places where he uses the word. Actually, *sphragis* appears in only one other of the genuinely Pauline letters, and it confirms our analysis of what Paul is talking about. In his first letter to the community in Corinth, Paul wrote

> Although I may not be an apostle to others, surely I am one to you.
> For you are the seal of my being an apostle in the Lord.
> (1 Corinthians 9:2)

Paul is arguing that his mission to the Corinthians is living proof of his being an apostle. They are the visible sign of his apostleship, which is something that cannot be seen simply by looking at him.

The two other places where *sphragis* is used in this way are in the Letter to the Ephesians, probably not written by Paul but long attributed to him. The first uses very Pauline language:

> You trusted in Christ when you heard the good news of your salvation. When you believed, you received the seal of that salvation, the promised holy spirit, which is the pledge of what we are to inherit until it is fully received, to the praise of his glory.
> (Ephesians 1:13–14)

The author here saying that when the Ephesians believed the good news of their salvation, they received a sign of it, namely the holy spirit that was manifested in charisms such as those demonstrated by the Corinthians and others. (See, for example, Acts 2:4, 8:17–18, 10:45–47, 19:2–6.) This letter also echoes the claim made in 2 Corinthians that the spiritual gifts that have been received are a pledge of more to come.

A little later, the author of Ephesians goes on to say,

> Do not sadden God's holy spirit, whose seal you bear until the day of redemption. (Ephesians 4:30)

Again, the seal of the spirit is the outward manifestation of what has been inwardly received.

These four references to the outward sign (*sphragis*) of an inner spirit remained relatively unnoticed and undiscussed for three centuries, until Augustine wrote about baptism late in the fourth century.

Augustine was the bishop of Hippo (on the coast of present-day Algeria) at a time when Christians in North Africa were divided over the issue of rebaptism. From the earliest days, Christians understood that baptism bestowed God's spirit on believers. We have just seen evidence of this in Corinthians and Ephesians. Three centuries later, baptism no longer resulted in the display of charismatic gifts such as speaking in tongues, but the belief that baptism bestowed the Holy Spirit was as strong as ever. One theological question that had not yet been resolved was whether it was possible to lose the spirit that had been received in baptism.

For over a century, many church leaders in North Africa followed the example of Donatus, a bishop who argued that heretics (who deny Christian doctrine) and apostates (who give up their faith) lost the Holy Spirit and therefore had to be rebaptized if they wanted to rejoin the church. Others followed the example of the church across the Mediterranean, which did not rebaptize those who had left the church. Instead, the practice in southern Europe was to offer reconciliation to those who repented of their error and wanted to rejoin the Christian community. Augustine was a member of this latter group.

Convinced that the practice of the Christian majority was correct, Augustine set himself the task of finding a proof for it. Searching the scriptures he came across the four passages cited above, but since he was unaware that the passages originally referred to morally converted and charismatic behavior, he interpreted them as referring to something metaphysical and unseen. On the basis of these texts, Augustine concluded what when converts are baptized they receive not only the Holy Spirit but also a spiritual seal (*sphragis*) that marks them as belonging to Christ. Repeatedly, Augustine invoked the analogy of a mark or brand that is put on sheep to show who owns them. Even if the sheep stray or are stolen, they never lose visible sign of their true owner.

In the same way, Augustine argued, the seal marks the baptized as belonging to Christ, and even if they leave the church they never lose the invisible sign that marks them as Christians. Therefore the practice of not rebaptizing is correct, because it would only be the equivalent of putting the same brand on an animal that was already branded. This is why the lapsed are received back into the church when they have repented of having gone astray, but they are not rebaptized. They lose the Holy Spirit when they leave the church, and they are once again joined to the Holy Spirit when they rejoin the body of Christ, but they never lose the invisible seal on their soul.

To be fair to Augustine, the texts from Corinthians and Ephesians that I have translated above are more ambiguous in the original Greek than I have made them out to be. Without an awareness of the charismatic behavior that characterized early conversions in the Jesus movement, it would be quite easy to interpret the passages referring to a visible sign as referring to an invisible sign. Part of Augustine's genius was that he could find an answer to a theological problem in the Bible that was the equivalent of finding a needle in a haystack. And Augustine's answer was so clear and insightful that it found a permanent place in the Catholic theology of baptism.

✶

Is it "holy spirit" or "Holy Spirit"?

You may have noticed in the preceding sections that references to the Holy Spirit are sometimes capitalized and sometimes not.

An explanation is in order.

✶

A common metaphor in the New Testament is spirit.

It all begins with the Greek word, *pneuma*. Like its Hebrew counterpart, *ruah* (You can pronounce ḥ like the ch in Bach.), *pneuma* originally meant breath, like the air that one inhales and exhales, but in time the word was used as a metaphor meaning spirit, or that which animates a living being. In the first chapter of Genesis, for example, when you read in translation that "the Spirit of God moved upon the face of the waters," the Hebrew word behind it is *ruah*.

Limiting our discussion to the New Testament, we can say that the metaphor of spirit is used to talk about a wide range of human behavior. The gospel writers talk about antisocial and other undesirable types of behavior in terms of evil spirits or unclean spirits. Today we might talk about such behavior in terms of mental illness or emotional disturbance, but the science of psychology was unknown in Jesus' day. Lacking any genuine insight into the cause of such behavior, it was described as though some spirit had taken over the person's actions.

In all likelihood, people in those days believed their own metaphors. That is, they believed that such spirits were real and were causing the mischief that others could observe. In other words, people in ancient times believed that people's behavior could be explained as the influence of spiritual beings—metaphysical realities in the root meaning of that term. The

Greek prefix *meta* means beyond, and the noun *physis* refers to the realm of physical or material reality. It's the word that was used to name the science of physics. Metaphysics deals with things beyond the realm of the physical.

Today most of us do not give much credence to biblical talk about evil spirits and unclean spirits. Unless we are fundamentalists, we do not believe that such things are real, even though we are sure that uncontrollable, antisocial and malicious types of behavior are real. Most Christians do, however, believe that good spirits are real, especially one in particular, namely the Holy Spirit.

In the New Testament, however, the Holy Spirit is a metaphor. Or rather, the Greek phrase *pneuma hagion*, or holy spirit, is used in the same way that the phrase *pneuma poneron*, or evil spirit, is used. It is used to name the unseen cause of good or godly behavior, just as *pneuma poneron* is used to name the unseen cause of bad or wicked behaviorr.

✶

At this point, more needs to be said about language.

Here are two things you should know about ancient Greek. The first is that words could be written in all capital letters, called majuscule, or in all small letters, called minuscule. The beginning of the Greek alphabet written in majuscule looks like this: Α Β Γ Δ Ε. The beginning of the Greek alphabet written in minuscule looks like this: α β γ δ ε. The oldest Greek copies of the New Testament are majuscule editions. Greek minuscule was not introduced until the ninth century. The point is that neither form of Greek had any way to capitalize proper names, so it could not write "*Pneuma Hagion.*" It was either "*PNEUMA HAGION*" or "*pneuma hagion*" in every copy of the Bible.

The second important thing to know is that the Greek language as spoken and written in biblical times does not have an indefinite article. English, by contrast, has both a definite article, "the," and an indefinite article, "a." If I want to talk about a particular book, for example, I write or say, "the book," but if I am referring to no book in particular, I write or say, "a book." In ancient Greek, when talking about a particular book, one says *to biblion*, or "the book." But when referring to no book in particular, one writes or says *biblion*, without a preceding article. It is usually translated as "a book."

35

Perhaps this is a good time to throw in some interesting facts about the Latin language as well. Latin has neither a definite article nor an indefinite article, so to know how a noun is being used, one needs to know the context. The Latin word for book is *liber*, and depending on the context in which the word is used, *liber* is translated as "book," "a book," or "the book."

Although ancient Latin, of the type found on old Roman monuments, used only majuscule letters (what we call capital or upper-case letters), medieval Latin used both. Hence, it could use capital letters to mark the beginnings of sentences and to indicate proper names.

✶

Let's get back to the New Testament and *pneuma hagion*.

It turns out that in about half the places where that phrase appears, the definite article is missing. Normally, one would translate *pneuma hagion* as "a holy spirit." But if you look at any English translation of the New Testament, the phrase is regularly translated as "the Holy Spirit."

How did this happen?

I am not a historian of language nor an expert in biblical manuscripts, but I can give you an educated guess.

During the first few centuries of Christianity, dogmas of faith were not yet defined. For example, some early followers of Jesus believed that he was a prophet, like the prophets in the Old Testament. Others believed that he was a special messenger sent from heaven, the way angels were believed to be sent by God to deliver messages to people on earth. Those who believed that Jesus was divine gave different interpretations of his divinity, for example, he was divine before his incarnation on earth but less than God, or he was made divine by God some time during his lifetime, or he was half human and half divine, and so on. In the early days, there was a variety of christologies, or interpretations of Jesus as the anointed one.

A number of factors accounted for this. Not every community of Christians had all the documents that comprise the New Testament. When Paul wrote his letters to the communities he evangelized, for example, none of the gospels had been written yet. And Paul's authentic letters (Ones written after he died around AD 66 were attributed to him, and some of these eventually made it into the New Testament.) have a relatively low christology, in other words, Paul did not speak of Jesus as divine.

❧

Furthermore, the gospels of Mark, Matthew and Luke were written for separate communities some time after Paul's martyrdom in Rome. It would have taken a while for Christians around the Roman Empire to obtain copies of all three gospels. Mark's christology is very low, and the other two are relatively low. In Matthew and Luke, Jesus is portrayed as miraculously born, as someone with extraordinary powers, and as raised from the dead, but he is never identified with the God whom Jesus called Father.

In contrast, John's gospel contains a very high christology, portraying Jesus as the pre-existent Word of God who clearly identifies himself with God the Father during the Last Supper. John was not written until the end of the first century at the earliest, however. Some of the later epistles and the book of Revelation also contain high christologies.

Lastly, there were other gospels, collections of Jesus' teachings, and other early Christian documents written during the first centuries that never made it into the New Testament. The list of 27 scrolls or books that today we call the New Testament first appeared in the middle of the second century and was not finalized by church officials until the fourth century.

During the first three centuries, then, Christians could hold to a low, medium or high christology and not be considered heretics. Indeed, the very first ecumenical council, held in Nicaea in AD 325, was convened to decide what the official teaching about Jesus should be. As can be seen in the Nicene Creed, it decided on a very high christology.

All through this time, however, the status of what was called the spirit of God, the spirit of Christ, and the Holy Spirit were left undecided. Finally, in 381, the Council of Constantinople condemned those who held that the Holy Spirit was not divine, adding to the Nicene Creed that the Spirit proceeds from the Father and is worshiped as God with the Father and the Son.

The above are all historical facts. What follows is my educated guess about what was going on behind the scenes.

During the centuries just referred to, both Latin and Greek were written in majuscule, and by the late fourth century Latin-speaking churchmen were thinking of *SPIRITUS SANCTUS* as referring to the Third Person of the Blessed Trinity, and the Greek-speaking churchmen were thinking of *PNEUMA HAGION* in the same way. It seems plausible, therefore, that when Latin began to be written in a combination of majuscule and minuscule, with proper names being capitalized, theologians in medieval universities found *Spiritus Sanctus* in their copies of the New Testament.

The same transition in spelling did not occur in biblical Greek. When manuscripts began to be written in minuscule, proper names were usually not capitalized, and even the Greek words for Lord and God were not capitalized. Eastern theologians, however, continued to treat *pneuma hagion* as referring to the Holy Spirit, despite the fact that the definite article is absent in almost half the places where those words appear in the New Testament.

So even the Holy Spirit started out as a metaphor and ended up as a metaphysical entity.

∗

Salvation was not always something that happened in heaven.

The word "salvation" appears over 40 times in English translations of the New Testament. Although the word can be interpreted to mean something that happens in the afterlife, there are clearly times when this is not the case.

At the beginning of Luke's gospel, a heavenly messenger reveals to Zechariah that his wife Elizabeth will bear a son who will be great in the eyes of God because he will turn people away from their sins and put them on a path to righteousness. When his son John (who would later be called the Baptist) is born, Zechariah bursts into a hymn of praise and thanks God for fulfilling the promise of the prophets to bring "salvation from our enemies and from the hands of those who hate us" (Luke 1:71) Apparently, Zechariah was thinking that his son would have something to do with a *meshiach* who would be instrumental in rescuing Israel from the oppressive rule of the Roman Empire. Salvation in this context would have to be something that happens in this life, not the next.

Likewise, during his encounter with Zacchaeus, a tax collector who renounces his dishonest practices and promises to share his wealth, Jesus proclaims, "Today salvation has come to this house" (Luke 19:9). Clearly, salvation here means something that is happening now, not something that Zacchaeus has to wait for.

In many other places, the word "salvation" is ambiguous, as it would have to be in order to be interpreted as having to do with heaven.

The problem is that most Jews in Jesus' day did not believe in an afterlife. The sect called the Pharisees did, perhaps under the influence of religious ideas from Persia. (During the so-called Babylonian captivity, Jews lived in Persia for many decades before being allowed to return home.) Paul had been a Pharisee before becoming a Christian, so it was easy for him to accept the idea of resurrection from the dead. Even for Paul, however, salvation is something that begins in this life.

The Latin for this word, *salvatio*, is related to the word *salus*, which basically means health, but which could be extended metaphorically to mean welfare, well-being, or even safety. The Greek word behind it is *sōteria*, which primarily means safety, preservation, or deliverance. In ordinary usage, then, salvation meant being preserved or rescued from something dangerous or harmful.

Along these same lines, the words "save" and "saved" appear between 90 and 100 times in the New Testament, depending on which translation you are reading. Often the word refers to rescuing from danger, as when the apostles are afraid of drowning (Matthew 8:25, 14:30), it contrasts saving life with taking life (Mark 3:4), and the word is used to taunt Jesus when he is hanging on the cross (Luke 23:35–39). "Save" can also mean to keep or preserve, as in saving the best wine until last (John 2:10) or saving perfume for a special purpose (John 12:7).

Most often, however, the verb "save" (in Greek *sōzō*, in Latin *salvo*) is used metaphorically and refers to being rescued from a moral danger rather than a physical one. This use is found especially in the Acts of the Apostles. On Pentecost, Peter tells the crowd, "Save yourselves from this corrupt generation" (Acts 2:40), members of the early Christian community were called "those who were being saved" (2:47), and people ask the apostles what they must do "to be saved" (16:30). They are told to "believe in the Lord Jesus" (16:31), which evangelical Christians interpret as meaning that they should accept a high christology and acknowledge Jesus as a divine being.

As we have seen however, a high christology became standard only in the fourth century. What then might salvation have looked like in the first century?

If most Jews did not believe in an afterlife, what might the writers of the gospels and epistles have been referring to when they spoke about salvation and being saved? Even the Pharisee Paul did not believe in heaven and hell the way later Christians did. Rather, he believed that there would be a resurrection of the dead, as Christ had risen from the dead, for those who had died in Christ, that is, for those who had died in the Christian community (See 1 Corinthians 15:12–21, 52). But Paul also speaks metaphorically about being raised. In his letter to the Romans, he says that Christ was raised from the dead by the Father so that "we too might live a new life" (Romans 6:4) and so that "we might bear fruit for God" (7:4), which is a metaphorical way of talking about doing what is right. The Epistle to the Colossians repeats this theme when it talks about being buried with Christ in baptism and "raised with him through your faith in the power of God, who raised him from the dead" (Colossians 2:12). What the author seems to be referring to is what members of Alcoholics Anonymous talk about when they talk about a power higher than themselves, a power that they can experience as giving them the strength to resist temptation and to remain sober. If this is a plausible interpretation, then Paul and the other epistle writers were talking out of their own experience when they talked about being raised to new life.

As it turns out, believing in the Lord Jesus, referred to above in Acts 16:31, can also be translated as having faith in Jesus the Master. The Greek word *pisteuo* can be translated as either "believe" or "have faith," in other words, to trust. What Peter in Acts is saying, therefore, and what Paul says in a number of places, is in effect, "Believe Jesus and have faith in the way of life that he made possible, and you will be raised from the sinful way you used to live because you can avail yourself of a spiritual power that comes from God. And the way to do this is in Christ, that is, in the community of believers who are animated by God's spirit. But to do so, you must be baptized, that is, you must be immersed in the community in order to share that spirit." If you have ever been a member of a group or club or team that has shared a common spirit, you understand the kind of thing that is being talked about here.

The ambiguity of Greek words like *pisteuō*, *sōzō* and *sōteria* made it possible for Christian beliefs to evolve from ideas rooted in experience to ideas that were given a metaphysical interpretation. Believing in Christ in order to be saved became a magical guarantee of going to heaven, as did the idea of having to be baptized in order to be saved. There are many passages in the New Testament that exhibit this ambiguity—many too many to be listed here—but it is good to offer a sample by way of illustration.

First, salvation can be interpreted as referring to a moral transformation that can be experienced or to a spiritual benefit that can be accepted on faith.

"All people will see God's salvation." (Luke 3:6)
"This message of salvation has been sent to us." (Acts 13:26)

"The power of God brings salvation to all who believe."
(Romans 1:16)

"Godly sorrow brings a change of heart that leads to salvation."
(2 Corinthians 7:10)

"Work out your salvation in fear and trembling." (Philemon 2:12)

Next, being saved can be interpreted as a moral transformation that is empowered by an energy that comes from God through a supportive community or as a spiritual transformation that will be rewarded by God in the future.

"The one who endures until the end will be saved." (Matthew 24:13)

"The disciples said to one another, "Who then can be saved?"
(Mark 10:26)

"The devil comes and changes their hearts so they do not believe and are not saved." (Luke 8:12)

"I am the gate. Anyone who enters through me will be saved."
(John 10:9)

"Through the grace of our Lord Jesus we are saved." (Acts 15:11)

"Everyone who calls on the name of the Lord will be saved."
(Romans 10:13)

"By this gospel you are saved." (1 Corinthians 15:2)

"It is by grace you have been saved through faith." (Ephesians 2:8)

"God wants all people to be saved." (1 Timothy 2:4)

*

Part of the confusion comes from passages about eternal life.

Reading about eternal life in the New Testament certainly gives the impression that the authors were talking about living for a long, long time—in fact, eternally. As we have seen, life after death was not a common idea in first century Palestine, and the only way that a person could possibly live forever would be by continuing to live in some fashion after he or she had died.

Could there be another way of interpreting the words that are translated as eternal life? As it happens, there is.

The ordinary Greek word for life is *bios*. It's the word that was used to name biology, the study of living things. But the word used in the New Testament is *zōē*, which basically meant a means of living (like an income

41

or a job) but which by extension meant life. The words "zoo" and "zoology" are derived from *zōē*. The Latin word *vita* basically means life, but the word could also be used metaphorically to mean vitality (which contains the Latin word as its root) or liveliness. Stretching the meaning of a word without changing it happens in English as well. If you are not dead, you must be living, but if you're having a great time, that's really living!

Let us look now at the words that are taken to mean eternal. The English word is actually a transliteration from the Latin *aeterna* rather than a translation. The prefix a-, in Latin as in English, can sometimes be what is technically known as an alpha privative, and it means not, as in the words "agnostic," "asymmetrical," and "asexual." There is no Latin word *terna*, but there is a Greek word that is similar to that, and it means limit or end or boundary. The Latin word *terminus* and the English word "terminal" are derived from the Greek noun *terma*, meaning boundary or end point. And the Greek *atermōn* is an adjective meaning boundless. So "eternal" and *aeterna* are related to *atermōn*, which originally meant the absence of a physical boundary, but which by derivation could mean the absence of an ending, or endless, hence, eternal. Metaphors again!

The Greek noun *aiōn*, which gets transliterated into English as "eon," means an age or a long time, and the adjective *aiōnia*, although it can mean eternal, can also mean lasting. Thus *zōē aiōnia*, although it is taken to mean eternal life in virtually all translations of the New Testament, can also mean unbounded life or lasting vitality, an unquenchable means of living. So the question becomes one of reference. To what were the scripture writers referring when they used the words, *zōē aiōnia*?

We have two clues. The first clue, as we have already noted, is that Jews in the first century (and the first followers of Jesus were all Jews) did not believe in life after death. Unless one believes that life goes on after death, *zōē aiōnia* cannot mean living for ever and ever. The second clue is something we discussed in chapter one, namely, that words arise out of experience. So we need to look for some experience that is full of energy and is long lasting.

The earliest mention of *zōē aiōnia* is in Paul's letter to the Galatians, written early in his career as an apostle. It is usually translated something like this:

> The one who sows for his flesh will reap corruption from the flesh, but the one who sows for the spirit will reap eternal life from the spirit. (Galatians 6:8 NABRE)

This is very metaphorical language to be sure, using agricultural images of sowing and reaping. But what is Paul talking about? I would suggest that the following translation gets closer to what Paul meant:

> Those who are motivated by natural desires will discover that they wither away, but those who opt for the spiritual life will discover boundless vitality. (Galatians 6:8)

Paul talking about things for which there is not a ready-made Greek vocabulary, so he stretches the meanings of words and speaks in terms of analogies, in this case, images taken from farming.

How did Paul know this? If he knew what he was talking about, he must have experienced it himself, or he must have seen others experiencing it, or both.

Paul does not speak about *zōē aiōnia* in his letters to the Corinthians, so it may not have been part of his customary vocabulary, even though a charismatic community is typically full of boundless vitality, at least in the early stages of the community's life. If you have been a member of a charismatic prayer group or Pentecostal church, you know what I am talking about.

So the only other place where Paul uses the words is in his letter to the Romans, written late in his career.

> To those who persevere in doing good, seeking to do what is always praiseworthy and honorable, God will give boundless vitality. (Romans 2:7)

Have you ever felt energized by doing good and helping others? Then you know what Paul is talking about.

Paul ends chapter 6 in Romans this way. First, the more usual way of translating that passage:

> But now that you have been freed from sin and have become slaves of God, the benefit that you have leads to sanctification, and its end is eternal life. For the wages of sin is death, but the gift of God is eternal life in Christ Jesus our Lord. (Romans 6:22–23 NABRE)

It is hard to picture what Paul is talking about here, or to figure out how he knows this. The following translation makes it easier to envision these things.

> Now that you have been liberated from sinful living and have become obedient to what God wants, you reap the benefit of holiness

43

and the result is boundless vitality. The wage paid by sinfulness is lifelessness, but the gift of God is boundless vitality in the community of Jesus, who is our teacher and master. (Romans 6:22–23)

In the Gospel of Mark, the next New Testament book in chronological order, the words *zōē aiōnia* appear only twice. In the first passage, a man runs up to Jesus and asks,

Good master, what should I do in order to acquire boundless vitality? (Mark 10:17)

Jesus tells him to keep the commandments, and when the man objects that he has already done that, Jesus suggests that he sell everything he has, give it to the poor, and follow him. The man in the story cannot accept this and he walks away sad, but there was a man in the thirteenth century who took Jesus at his word, gave everything to the poor, and found happiness that lasted the rest of his life. His name was Giovanni Bernardone, but most people know him as St. Francis of Assisi. If you have read about the life of St. Francis, you know he had boundless vitality.

The twenty-fifth chapter of Matthew's Gospel contains the famous parable of the sheep and the goats, symbolically those who do God's will those who do not. In the very last verse of the chapter, the wicked are sent off to be punished without limits and the just are set aside to receive life without limits. But it does not say that either group will live forever.

Luke's Gospel cites a version of the story cited above in Matthew, but it also contains a story not found in any other gospel. The story of the Good Samaritan (Luke 10:25–37) is too familiar to be repeated here, but most of us overlook the fact that it begins with the same question that starts off Mark's story of the rich man in chapter 10: "What should I do in order to acquire boundless vitality?" In this case the answer is love your enemies. Quakers and other Christians who renounce war understand what Jesus is talking about here. It is a great relief not to hate people.

John's Gospel is full of references to *zōē aiōnia*, seventeen in fact, and by the end of the first century when the gospel was written for a Greek audience, the words were beginning to be interpreted as referring to eternal life or living forever. Still, in most of the verses in which the phrase appears, it can be interpreted as referring to unbounded life or lasting vitality. Check it out for yourself in John 3:15–16, 3:36, 4:14, 5:24, 6:27, 6:47, 6:68, 12:50, and 17:2–3.

By the fourth century, however, Christians were no longer Jews who accepted Jesus as *meshiach*, but Greeks who believed that human beings could be divine, and who believed in life after death. This is not the place to explain how Jesus became understood as the Son of God and the Second Person of the Blessed Trinity. Our focus is on the sacraments, and on how words and phrases that originally had an experiential meaning and a reference to real life were given a metaphysical meaning referring to what went on in the soul quite apart from ordinary experience.

✶

There are metaphors in the story of the Last Supper.

The earliest account of Jesus' last meal with his disciples is not in any of the gospels but in Paul's first letter to the Corinthians, written around the year 55. After he had left the Greek city of Corinth to continue his missionary work, Paul received word that there was dissension and disorganization in the community, which at the time was probably a few dozen people at most. Among the problems he addressed was people's conduct at the weekly community meal, which he called the Lord's supper. This is what he wrote in chapter 11, verses 20–34:

> When you gather together, it is not the Lord's supper that you eat, for there are those who eat their food before the others can eat, so that some go hungry while others are drunk. Don't you have your own houses to eat and drink in? In God's assembly, is it right to belittle and shame the poor? What can I say to you? Should I praise you? Certainly not!
>
> What I passed on to you is what I received from the Lord, namely, that on the night he was betrayed, the Lord Jesus took bread, gave thanks, broke it, and said, "Take and eat. This is my body that is broken for you. Do this and remember me." Likewise, he took the cup after supper and said, "This cup is the new covenant in my blood. As often as you drink from it, remember me."
>
> As often as you eat this bread and drink this cup, you are proclaiming the death of the Lord until he comes. Therefore, anyone who eats this bread or drinks the cup unworthily will be accountable for the body and blood of the Lord.
>
> People should ask themselves, when they eat the bread and drink the cup, whether they are eating and drinking unworthily, so that no one can say that they are not recognizing the body of the Lord.

This is why many of you are sick and weak, and many have fallen asleep. If we were more mindful, we would not suffer such judgment. But when the Lord does pass such judgment on us, it is to correct us and to keep us from being condemned with the world.

Brothers and sisters, when you gather together for a meal, wait for one another before eating. If you are really hungry at the time, eat something at home before coming. This way, you will do nothing wrong. With regard to any other matters, I will address them the next time I come.

This passage contains both symbols and metaphors.

It was common for the followers of Jesus to come together for a weekly fellowship meal, following the practice of Jewish rabbis who had a weekly supper with their disciples. Since Jesus was considered a teacher or rabbi, there is a good chance that he followed this practice even though it is not mentioned in the gospels. Paul gives it the symbolic name, "Lord's Supper," which he probably learned from other Christians. The name signified that it was not an ordinary meal but one in which Jesus and his teachings were remembered.

When Paul says that he learned about the Last Supper "from the Lord," he may be using a metaphor. If he considered the Christian community to be a manifestation of the risen Christ, then learning about Jesus' last meal from those who received him after his conversion could have been, in his mind, the same as learning about it from the Master himself.

Paul quotes words of Jesus that are most likely symbolic. Although later Christians came to believe that Jesus wrought a metaphysical change in the bread and wine at the Last Supper, and that priests had the power to produce the same metaphysical change in bread and wine, it is unlikely that Jesus or his earliest followers were thinking in these terms. The Torah forbade the drinking of blood, and Jews were accustomed to eating symbolic foods during their Passover supper.

There is also a linguistic argument against taking these words of Jesus literally. In the original Greek and in the Latin translations of this verse and parallel verses in the gospels, a copula appears between "this" and "my body" and between "this" and "my blood." In Greek, the first sentence reads, *Touto mou estin to sōma*, and it Latin it reads *Hoc est corpus meum*. The Greek copula *estin* and the Latin copula *est* are translated in English as "is," so the sentence literally reads, "This is my body."

Although the gospels and epistles were written in Greek, Jesus did not speak Greek but Aramaic, which can be considered a dialect of Hebrew. Speaking Aramaic at the Last Supper, Jesus would have said the equivalent of "This my body" and "This my blood," without any copula in the middle. Thus it is impossible to know from the words he used whether Jesus meant to say that the bread and wine were actually his body and blood, or whether they symbolized his body and blood. But because of the Jewish prohibition against drinking blood, it is most likely that he meant the words to be taken symbolically.

Paul next says that those who partake of the bread and wine proclaim the death of the Lord. Did he mean this literally or metaphorically? The Christians in Corinth knew that Jesus had been crucified, so why would they need to proclaim it to themselves? The Greek verb here is *katangelō*, in which you can find the English word "angel," and *angelos* is Greek for messenger.

What was it, then, that Paul wanted the Corinthians to remember when they gathered for the Lord's supper? He calls it "the death of the Lord," but if those words do not refer literally to Jesus' physical death 20 years earlier, to what might they refer metaphorically?

From the passage quoted above, it is clear that some members of the community were acting selfishly. The Lord's supper was apparently akin to what we call a pot luck supper, where everyone brings something to share. But instead of waiting for everyone to arrive, those who came early were eating up all the food and not leaving anything for those who came later. (Remember in those days there were no clocks, so the hours of the day were always approximate. It would have been easy to come early or to come late.)

We have already seen, when reviewing Paul's teachings on baptism, that he interpreted the immersion in water as immersion in the death of Christ. In Paul's mind, Jesus' death was anything but selfish, for he died in obedience to God's will, giving of himself that others might live the way God intended. Those who accepted baptism, immersion in the body of Christ, symbolically proclaimed that they were dead to sin, which included things like greed and selfishness.

Paul's mention of the death of the Lord is therefore most likely a metaphorical reference to renouncing sinful habits and accepting God's will, which in this case meant loving each other, as Paul would soon remind them in the next section of his letter (1 Corinthians 12–13).

If this interpretation is correct, then Paul's reference in the next paragraph to recognizing the body of the Lord most likely means recognizing that the community is collectively the body of Christ, and it is not likely to be a plea to acknowledge that the bread has been metaphysically transformed. It is a metaphorical reference, in other words, rather than a literal one.

This having been said, I do not think it is necessary to delve into the gospel accounts of the Last Supper, which contain the words of Jesus over the bread and wine but do not provide as much commentary as Paul does in his letter to the Corinthians.

For much the same reason, I do not think it is necessary to comment on John 6:35–58, which is often called the Bread of Life discourse. Christians from the fourth century onward, who believed that a metaphysical change occurs in the bread and wine used in the liturgy, often interpreted this passage literally. Thus when Jesus says in verse 51, "This bread is my flesh, which I will give for the life of the world," the words were taken as reinforcing a literal interpretation of Jesus' words at the Last Supper. But if those words are not taken literally, then there is no reason to give a literal interpretation to what Jesus says in the Bread of Life discourse. Given that John's is the most symbolic of the four gospels, it makes more sense to take the discourse as a metaphorical reference to the spiritual life, meaning that Christians ought to be internally nourished by the example and teachings of Jesus.

✶

The metaphor of sacrifice began to appear rather early in reference to Christian worship.

In the Epistle to the Hebrews, written some time in the first century for a community of Jews who had accepted the teachings of Jesus, his death on the cross was interpreted as a sacrifice or offering to God. This idea is also found in a few of Paul's letters and in letters originally ascribed to him, but it is not an image that was applied to the Lord's supper or to any other meals that Christians shared in memory of Jesus.

The Greek word that gets translated into "sacrifice" in English had two closely related meanings in the ancient world. A *thusia* could be an offering or gift made to a god, usually in a place of worship such as a temple or shrine. Secondly, *thusia* was the name given to the event that involved giving the gift or making the offering. When one participated in a *thusia*, therefore, one brought a *thusia* for the intended deity.

When *thusia* was rendered into Latin, it was translated as *sacrificium*, which conveyed the double meaning of *thusia* by combining two Latin words, *sacrum* and *facere*. *Sacrum* means sacred or holy, and *facere* means to make. A *thusia* made something sacred by consecrating it to a god, and this occurred during a holy-making event in a religious setting. Hence both the event and the gift were called a *sacrificium* in Latin.

It should be clear to see that the English word "sacrifice" is both a translation of *thusia* and a transliteration of *sacrificium*. In biblical and other ancient texts, what is offered is called a sacrifice, and the act of offering is also called a sacrifice.

With few exceptions, pagan sacrifices in the ancient world have included a meal. People brought food to the event, and if the food was an animal, it was ritually killed on the altar or in another designated space. After being cooked, part of the sacrifice was offered to the god (by destroying or removing it in some way), part of it was given to the officiating priests (a donation for their services), and the rest was shared by those who had come for the religious ritual. Thus sacrifices almost always entailed eating together.

The earliest known reference to a Christian meal as a *thusia* is in the *Didachē*, previously mentioned in this chapter, and possibly written late in the first century. The participants are admonished to confess their sins and be reconciled with one another so that their sacrifice will not be defiled. In those days, a sacrifice was considered pure if those offering it were ritually pure. For the Christians for whom the *Didachē* was written, this apparently meant being reconciled with all the other members of the community.

Prayers of thanksgiving (*eucharistia*) were said at the community meals, but the meal itself is given no special name. Interestingly, the *Didachē* makes no mention of the Last Supper, so the saying of what were later called the words of institution ("This is my body. . . . This is my blood.") does not seem to have been an essential part of these meals.

*

Christian ritual meals were called sacrifices in explanations to non-Christians.

For about three centuries, Christianity was not recognized as a religion by the Roman authorities. Accordingly, members of this growing religious movement were sometimes regarded with suspicion, and they were occasionally used as scapegoats when authorities needed someone to blame. In the mid-sixties, for instance, Nero blamed the Christians for a fire that consumed a large area in Rome, and in the subsequent persecution, the apostles Peter and Paul were martyred. For the most part, though, Christians were free to practice and even spread their faith, although they were sometimes considered disloyal because they did not worship the Roman gods or pay religious tribute to the Roman emperor.

To counteract such suspicions, a Christian named Justin (who was later martyred) wrote about what Christians do at their weekly worship. He was attempting to refute the accusation that the followers of Jesus were atheists because they did not behave like their pagan counterparts. In essence, Justin argued that the followers of Jesus held their sacrificial meals in homes rather than in temples and shrines.

As in the *Didachē*, the weekly meal is one in which thanks is offered to God for the special food that is shared by those in attendance. The noun *eucharistia*, meaning thanksgiving is used, and also its derivative verb form, meaning to give thanks. At this time in the mid-second century, the meal had apparently become a symbolic one with bread and wine instead of a full meal. Only those who have been baptized and who live according to the teachings of Jesus are allowed to partake, implicitly referring to the custom that only the devotees of particular gods were admitted to the rites honoring those gods. Justin explains that, just as ordinary bread and wine are changed when they provide physical nourishment, the bread and wine are changed into the body and blood of Christ in order provide spiritual nourishment.

Although Justin does not explicitly call the Christian meal a *thusia*, he argues that this ritual fulfills the prophesy found in the Old Testament book of Malachi, in which God speaking through the prophet says,

> Everywhere a pure sacrifice (*thusia kathara*) is offered to my name because my name is great among the nations, says the Lord almighty. (Malachi 1:11)

We have already seen that a pure sacrifice in the ancient world was one offered by those who had been purified, and since by this time there were Christians throughout the Roman world, it was clear to Justin that this passage referred to the Christian home ritual of giving thanks and sharing food.

About a half century later, Irenaeus of Lyon, in his book *Against Heresies*, also cited the verse from Malachi and took it as a direct reference to the Christian practice of offering to God bread and wine, which are understood to be the body and blood of Christ. Thus by the end of the second century, the weekly community meal was being likened to a sacrifice in the ancient sense of that term.

✶

In the third century, the metaphor became a metaphysical reality.

A pagan *thusia* or *sacrificium* ordinarily took place in a temple or shrine that contained an image of the god being venerated, usually a statue or mosaic picture. Thus the devotees who offered food to the god also shared their meal in the god's presence, symbolically speaking. In the Christian ritual, the presence of Christ was symbolized by bread and wine, and the presence of these symbols would have enabled the participants to experience the presence of Christ in a similar way.

Moreover, through the ritual of gift giving, the worshipers of pagan gods expressed their devotion to the gods and the values they represented, whether it was motherly devotion, romantic love, or courage in battle. Through giving a gift, they symbolically gave of themselves, as is the case when anyone gives a gift. This is why, if someone rejects a present we have offered, we ourselves feel a sense of rejection.

Since most of the people who became followers of Jesus during the first three centuries were adults, they would have understood the spiritual dynamic of sacrificial rites, and they would have brought that understanding to the Christian practice of offering sacred bread and wine to God, and then sharing that food and drink with one another. In other words, instead of Christian worship being likened to sacrificial practices, Christian worship became a sacrificial practice.

This understanding is quite clear in the writings of Cyprian of Carthage, a bishop in North Africa. Cyprian took the sacrificial imagery found in the Epistle to the Hebrews and applied it to Christian worship, understood as a sacrifice. The author of this epistle spoke of Jesus as a high priest who offered the perfect sacrifice—himself—to God as a once-and-for-all atonement for sins (Hebrews 5:1–10; 7:26–28; 9:11–15, 23–28; 10:1–18).

Hebrews interprets the death of Jesus through the metaphor of priesthood as understood in the Old Testament and the practice of offering sacrifices to God in atonement for sins. Cyprian, however, took this metaphor literally as something that happened in the realm beyond physical space and time, that is, he took it as a metaphysical reality. But Cyprian also went further in that he saw this metaphysical reality as something that occurred during Christian worship:

> For if Jesus Christ our Lord and God is himself the high priest of God the Father, and he first gave himself as an offering (*sacrificium*) to the Father, and then commanded this to be done in his memory, certainly the priest who imitates what Christ did truly serves in the place of Christ, and he makes in the church a true and complete offering (*sacrificium*) to God the Father when he proceeds to offer what he sees Christ himself offered. (Letter 63, chapter 14)

By the end of the third century, then, at least in the minds of some church leaders whose writings would become influential in the future, Christian worship was something that occurred in this world and also in a metaphysical realm. The actions of a priest imitate Christ the high priest, and so he offers to God the same sacrifice that Jesus offered to God on the cross.

*

Once the metaphors were believed to be metaphysical realities, there was no turning back.

In the fourth century, Christianity became part of the establishment. For a number of decades, the Roman Empire had been divided into two administrative regions, one in the West centered in Rome and one in the East centered in Byzantium (present-day Istanbul). Even so, the Empire was beset by problems within and without. Barbarian tribes harassed the borders, and Roman generals fought among themselves. Finally, in the year 312, a general named Constantine succeeded in defeating most of his rivals and sought to unify the Empire by promoting a single religion for all. Legends surround his selection of Christianity, but the fact remains that in 313 he issued an edict making Christianity one of the legally recognized religions in the Roman Empire.

It is also a fact that Constantine actively promoted Christianity, hoping that it would supplant the old Greco-Roman religion of gods and goddesses as well as the myriad local and household deities that today we would consider folk religion. He declared the Day of the Sun to be a day of rest in honor of Christ's resurrection, and he turned public buildings called basilicas (from the Greek word *basileus*, meaning king or emperor) over to the Christians for their Sunday worship. Later, when Christians began building places of worship for themselves, they copied the basilica style of a long building with a high ceiling down the middle supported by two rows of columns.

The weekly Christian gathering, which had migrated from evening to morning over the course of centuries, had until then taken place primarily in the large homes of the wealthier members of the community. Transferring the ritual meal into a public building on a weekly holiday made it possible, in the minds of church leaders, to honor God in the way gods deserved to be honored—with processions and chanting, with torches and incense, with multiple ministers wearing special vestments, and with sacred vessels made of precious metals. To get a sense of what Christian worship looked like in the fourth century, you need only attend a Greek Orthodox liturgy, because it has not changed much since then (except that it is a lot shorter today).

Once Christians around the empire could openly practice their religion and discuss their faith with one another, unexpected differences began to emerge. As mentioned earlier, there were a number of christologies ranging from fairly low (e.g., Jesus was a prophet) to fairly high (e.g., Jesus was divine), and even among the high christologies there were those who believed that Jesus had been made divine by God and those who believed that Christ was equal in divinity to God the Father. Fearing that his vision of religious unity was in danger of disintegrating, Constantine summoned the world's bishops to a meeting at his summer villa in Nicaea near Byzantium, recently renamed Constantinople in honor of the emperor. He charged them with composing a statement of faith with which they could all agree, and the result was the Nicene Creed, which is still said in churches on Sundays (including parts about the Holy Spirit, which were added later).

Interestingly, the Creed said nothing at all about what Jesus had taught, beyond the idea that God is a Father. It therefore said nothing about loving one another, or forgiving each other, or sharing one's wealth, or helping the needy, or renouncing violence, or loving one's enemies. Moral conversion and spiritual gifts had been the focus of those who followed the teachings of Jesus during the first decades of the Christian movement, but now the focus was on what to believe rather than on how to behave. Typical of this attitude, Constantine became a Christian believer fairly early during his reign, but he was not baptized until shortly before he died. Politically, this was a shrewd move because he could present himself as a convert to his Christian subjects while demonstrating to his pagan subjects that he was not fully Christian. Indeed, he continued to wage war against his enemies for about ten years until they were all subdued.

Another reason why it made sense to Constantine to postpone his baptism was that by this time, the ritual of immersion in water was believed to forgive all the sins a person had committed up to that point in time. We have already seen that baptism during the first decades was said to bring about a new life in Christ and to remit the sins of the past. This initially meant starting a new life in the community of Jesus' followers and getting rid of one's sinful habits prior to the water ritual. Three centuries later, however, those words were taken to mean that baptism washed one's soul clean and infused it with the Holy Spirit. In psychological terms, this was an exercise in magical thinking, but it was not recognized as such at the time.

Thus, all the words and phrases we took time to interpret as based in experience at the beginning of this chapter had, by the fourth century, been given the metaphysical interpretations that they have had ever since.

*

The body and blood of Christ became central to Christian beliefs.

One way to summarize the shift in Christianity that occurred during the fourth century is to say that orthodoxy replaced orthopraxis. The Greek prefix *orthos* means straight or true (hence an orthodontist straightens your teeth), the word *doxa* means teaching or doctrine (and, in some contexts, praise, hence a doxology is a hymn of praise), and *praxis* means practice in the sense of action or activity. During the reign of Constantine, Christianity shifted from emphasizing doing what is right to thinking correctly about God, Jesus Christ, and eventually also, the Holy Spirit. When Christianity was declared the state religion of the Roman Empire in the year 380, the official decree insisted that everyone should accept the faith of the Christian bishops and that those who believed otherwise were insane heretics. The shoe was now on the other foot, and those who believed wrongly could be persecuted for their beliefs regardless of how moral or saintly they were.

We have already seen that *eucharistia*, meaning thanksgiving, characterized many of the prayers that were said at the Christian ritual meal during the first century. In time, the word lent itself to the entire ritual or liturgy, as public worship was called in the Christian Roman Empire. Sunday worship in Orthodox churches even today is called the divine liturgy, and in the Catholic Church it is called the eucharistic liturgy, even though it is more popularly called the mass—a word derived from the Latin *missa*, which Catholic worship has been called since the Middle Ages.

Perhaps this is a good place to point out that the Christian church in the Roman Empire was called both catholic and orthodox—orthodox meaning that the church taught the true doctrine and offered God true praise, and catholic from *kata holon*, literally according to the whole, meaning universal. When the Eastern and Western halves of the church split in the eleventh century, the Eastern or Greek-speaking churches took the name "Orthodox," and the Western or Latin-speaking church took the name "Catholic." Had it turned out otherwise, today we might be speaking of the Roman Orthodox Church and the Eastern Catholic churches. Changes in the use of words is partly what this book is about.

In the fourth century, however, theological language was still in flux. Public worship was referred to as the eucharist in the East and it was not yet called the mass in the West. For a long time, the bread and wine used in the liturgy had been called the body and blood of Christ after they were consecrated or made sacred. Eventually the consecrated elements were also called the Eucharist, so for the sake of clarity the word will be capitalized here when it refers to the body and blood of Christ, and it will not be capitalized when it refers to the liturgy. Unfortunately, the adjective "eucharistic" is never capitalized, showing that theology is not nearly as precise as we would like it to be.

Be that as it may, bishops in the fourth century began insisting that the bread and wine used in the liturgy become the body and blood of Christ. On the one hand, this was because of the universal church's new insistence on orthodoxy. On the other hand, it was because converts to Christianity no longer went through a long period of preparation before being baptized into the community. Now they were baptized first and instructed later. And the instruction was primarily doctrinal instruction.

Thus Cyril of Jerusalem urged the newly baptized not to believe their senses but to believe that the power of God can transform the eucharistic elements: "Do not judge the matter by taste, but by faith be fully assured that the body and blood of Christ have been granted to you" (Fourth Lecture on the Mysteries, paragraph 6). Similarly, Gregory of Nyssa taught, "In the dispensation of grace, Christ plants Himself in all the faithful by means of that flesh fashioned from wine and bread, blending Himself with the bodies of the faithful" (Catechetical Oration 37). Clearly these Eastern bishops were explaining that being a Christian meant believing in metaphysical realities.

Bishops in the West were equally insistent. Ambrose of Milan wrote,

> The Lord Jesus himself proclaims, "This is my body." Before the blessing of the heavenly words, something of a different nature is spoken of, but after the consecration, a body is referred to. He himself speaks of his blood. Before the consecration it is called something else, but after it is referred to as blood. And you say, "Amen," that is, "It is true."
> (*On the Mysteries*, chapter 9, paragraph 54)

And Augustine of Hippo, after explaining to the recently baptized that they had become members of the body of Christ, exhorted them to "Become what you see, and receive what you are," when they were about to receive the Eucharist during the liturgy (Sermon 272). Being members of the body of Christ and filled with God's spirit was no longer something that could be experienced, as it could be in the charismatic communities of early Christianity, so now it had to be believed in as a metaphysical reality.

3

Schoolmen and Science

LIFE IN THE MIDDLE Ages was hard.

You may have seen read or seen stories about the Crusades, about medieval knights and fair damsels, about actual wars between England and France, or about fictitious rivalries in the television series, "Game of Thrones," but none of that shows you what life was like for ordinary people. Without the advantages of modern science and technology, most people in Europe lived in houses made of stone and mud, with thatched roofs and rough hewn wood doors, with no glass for windows, with no stoves or refrigerators, and with no indoor plumbing. They sweltered in the summer and froze in the winter, not to mention having little to eat from early winter until the first spring crops could be harvested.

Some of the most civilized places to live, if you were not fortunate enough to belong to the nobility, were in monasteries and convents. Although monks and nuns gave up marriage, they gained the ability to live fairly comfortably without the threat of starvation since the men and women who lived in community pooled their resources. They could build together, farm together, and work together. They preserved practical knowledge that was all but lost after the fall of the Roman Empire in the fifth century—knowledge about weaving and tanning, pottery making and metal smithing, retaining the arts of food preservation and cooking, and of course, wine-making.

Some monasteries also preserved the literature of the ancient world. Scrolls of papyrus deteriorated quickly and had to be copied over and over if their knowledge was not to be lost. Even books handwritten on parchment, made from animal skins, did not last forever. Ink faded, and pages became brittle. Precious works such as the Bible and the fathers of the church from Justin to Augustine were given top priority. Next were the writings of ancient poets, historians and philosophers. But there were no works of science.

There had been some scientific activity in the ancient world, in the golden ages of Greece and Rome. Hippocrates and Galen had done research on medicines and on the preservation of health. Pythagoras had written works on mathematics. Both the Greeks and the Romans had made advances in architecture. And an Egyptian astronomer named Ptolemy had calculated how the sun, moon and planets moved through the heavens around a stable and stationary Earth.

Although this ancient science was unknown in medieval Europe, it was available in the Near East, at least for those who had the ability to read and the leisure to study. Then the Near East was overrun by Muslims during the expansion of Islamic empires beginning in the seventh century of the Christian era. By the eighth century, Muslim armies had conquered North Africa, crossed the Straits of Gibraltar, and established a caliphate in Spain. Although blocked from the rest of Europe by the Pyrenees Mountains and Christian armies, Muslims established schools and imported the knowledge of the ancient world into southern Europe, where Christians, Jews and Muslims lived together in relative harmony.

Among the writings imported from the Near East were Arabic translations of Greek works, including those of Aristotle, who had written about physics and metaphysics, astronomy and biology, rhetoric and logic, ethics and politics in a rather systematic fashion. Aristotle went beyond describing and cataloguing what he observed to inquiring about the origins and causes of things insofar as they could be understood with reason and logic. He was also interested in knowledge for its own sake rather than for its practical value. In Latin, such knowledge was called *scientia*, from which we get the English word, science. Until the beginning of modern science in the seventeenth century, the only way to understand things thoroughly and systematically was by using Aristotelian science.

Muslim intellectuals in Spain used Aristotelian logic when arguing with their Christian counterparts about religion. Not to be outdone, Christians got their hands on Arabic translations of Aristotle and translated them into Latin. Even though these translations of translations were not always clear or accurate, they increased Europeans' knowledge of the real world enormously. At the same time, they sometimes got Christian intellectuals in trouble, as when Berengar of Tours was condemned for his unorthodox explanation of the Eucharist based on Aristotelian logic.

Around the same time that medieval schools were developing into universities, Aristotle's works were translated into Latin from the original Greek, and these were clearly more accurate and usable to Christian scholars. The University of Paris, which was famous for its theology faculty, was one of the first to make use of the new translations. Those who taught in the schools were called *scholastici* or schoolmen, and the type of theology they developed was called scholasticism or scholastic theology.

✶

The schoolmen began the systematic study of Christian beliefs and practices.

First, texts that had been laboriously copied and recopied for centuries were brought into the university and sorted according to type. Next, excerpts were taken from the writings and grouped according to subject matter—doctrines such as the Incarnation and the Trinity, moral issues raised by the Ten Commandments, and church practices such as the sacraments. These collections of texts, not all of which agreed with each other, were then studied in an effort to arrive at a comprehensive understanding of the Christian faith in all its aspects. They were the first text books.

The word *sacramentum* in Latin meant literally a sacred sign or a sign of something sacred. In many ways, it was the equivalent of the English word, symbol. Many things in medieval Christianity were symbolic—the cross, images of Christ and the saints, religious feasts such as Christmas and Easter, priestly vestments, and church rituals such as baptism and the mass. Which of these should be studied scientifically, and how could it be done?

A text book by a schoolman named Peter Lombard proposed that seven *sacramenta* should be investigated because, unlike signs that simply represented sacred things (such as art work or Bible stories or religious feasts), there were some that produced spiritual effects. Baptism, for example, turned pagans into Christians, marriage or matrimony turned single individuals into a married couple, and ordination turned laymen into priests. Could Aristotelian science explain how these ritual signs produced their effects? Lombard collected texts from the scriptures and the fathers of the church on the seven *sacramenta* that, in his opinion, covered Christian life from birth to death: baptism, confirmation, the Eucharist, penance, marriage, ordination, and extreme unction or last anointing. From then on, when Roman Catholics talked about the *sacramenta* or sacraments in the church, they were referring to these seven. The rest became known as *sacramentalia*—sacramentals or sacrament-like.

The Aristotelian science that was used to study the sacraments was metaphysics—an obvious choice since sacraments involved both visible and invisible elements. Baptism, for example, was a visible ritual that had an effect on the soul, which was invisible.

The seven sacraments were well known in the European church by the thirteenth century, which was the high point of medieval scholasticism, when Alexander of Hales, Bonaventure and Thomas Aquinas were teaching and writing. Baptism was a ritual performed on children shortly after they were born. Confirmation was done by bishops on those who were older. The Eucharist, also called the body and blood of Christ, was produced during the mass. Priests heard confessions in the sacrament of penance. Extreme unction was received shortly before death. Matrimony united two people in wedlock. And holy orders were bestowed on various ranks of the clergy.

Well-known too were the effects of the sacraments. Baptism forgave original sin and enabled a person to receive the other sacraments. Confirmation strengthened the soul. The words of consecration, spoken by a priest at mass, turned bread and wine into the body and blood of Christ. Penance remitted both mortal and venial sins. Extreme unction prepared the soul for heaven. Matrimony created a spiritual bond between husband and wife. Ordination bestowed priestly powers on men.

The challenge before the schoolmen, therefore, was to understand how the sacraments produced the effects that they were known to have in the medieval church. In other words, they needed to come up with a scientific explanation of how they worked. That they worked was not in doubt; all Catholics from peasants to nobles, from the lowliest cleric to the pope himself, knew what the sacraments were and the role they played in medieval Christian life. The scientific task was to understand how they worked.

*

What was needed was a metaphysical explanation.

Aristotelian metaphysics contained a number of concepts for understanding the nature of reality. All physical things, for example, were composed of matter and form, which is to say, there is something sensible about them and something intelligible about them. As we saw in the first chapter, the senses perceive the physical aspect of things and the mind perceives the intelligible aspect of things. Everything in the world around us has both a material dimension and an intelligible dimension. In the philosophical shorthand of the day, they were composed of *materia* and *forma*, matter and form.

Analyzing further, any individual thing was a substance that had accidents. A table and chair, for example, were two different substances with two different sets of accidents. In words that make more sense to us today, they were two different things with two different sets of sensible qualities—color, texture, shape, and so on. But the same could be said of two different chairs. Even though they had the same form or intelligibility, they could differ in color, texture, shape, and so on, making them two individual chairs. Even if they looked exactly the same, they were still in two different places. In Aristotelian metaphysics, location was a quality or accident.

When the technical terms of Aristotelian metaphysics are explained in more familiar language, it becomes clear that what Aristotle was trying to do was to understand the basic features of what can be experienced in the real world. Because those basic features were not things in the ordinary sense of the term, but rather aspects of things, they were in that sense beyond what is physical, or metaphysical. Today we might call them explanatory concepts or mental constructs that ancient and medieval philosophers used to understand the world around them.

Medieval theologians, however, faced an additional challenge. Besides having to understand material realities, they also had to understand spiritual realities and how the two were able to interact. To do so, they had to come up with some new explanatory concepts.

In sacramental theology, the most important of these concepts was *sacramentum et res*, literally sacred sign and thing, but usually translated as sacramental reality. In Latin, a *res* was not necessarily a material thing; it could also refer to a spiritual reality, such as grace.

All sacraments were understood to confer God's grace, which is something real, and therefore a *res* in scholastic terminology. The word *gratia* in Latin, grace in English, basically means gift. The spiritual gifts about which Paul wrote to the Corinthians—speaking in tongues, prophesying, healing, and so on—are sometimes called charisms in English. The original Greek word is *charisma*, which was often translated as *gratia* in Latin, and which could be translated as grace in English.

But the various sacraments were also understood to confer something unique to each individual receiving the sacrament. Baptism conferred salvation, confirmation conferred a gift of the Holy Spirit, penance conferred the forgiveness of sins, and so on. What exactly was this thing that was unique to each sacrament, yet a gift or grace nonetheless?

Clues came from two directions. The first was the spiritual seal mentioned by Augustine as something received through baptism and never lost. Whatever it was, it was both a gift or grace and a sign of belonging to Christ. The second was the bread and wine that were consecrated at mass. Once consecrated by a priest, they were no longer bread and wine but the body and blood of Christ. At the same time, their appearance was a sign of the real presence of Christ.

If two sacraments conferred something that was a sign as well as a gift, could this possibly be true of all of them?

To understand why the scholastics said yes, this concept could be generalized and applied to all the sacraments, we need to understand something unique to Aristotelian metaphysics.

In human imagination, things can easily be changed into other things by magic or divine power. In the Book of Exodus, Moses casts down his rod and it turns into a snake. In folk tales, people get transformed into animals and vice-versa. In the genre of comic books, Peter Parker acquires superpowers by being bitten by a radioactive spider.

Aristotle observed that in the real world, however, things change only if they have the ability to change. Wood can be burned and changed into ashes, but iron is not able to do that. An acorn can become an oak tree, but a pebble cannot. A caterpillar can become a butterfly, but an earthworm does not have that ability.

From the perspective of Aristotelian science, therefore, a natural human soul could not see God in heaven without first being given the ability to do so. Human beings have natural powers, but the ability to see God is not one of them. Human beings can forgive offences committed against them, but they cannot naturally forgive offenses committed against others or against God. They do not have the power to do so.

In their experience of medieval Christianity, the schoolmen saw that priests have the ability to forgive sins and to change bread and wine into the body and blood of Christ. They also knew that before they were ordained, priests did not have these abilities. It was therefore obvious to the schoolmen that men received priestly powers through being ordained.

Reflection on ordination thus provided another piece of the puzzle. The metaphysical status of what was received through a sacramental ritual is that it was a supernatural power of some sort.

*

This implied that Christians were truly different from non-Christians.

When babies were baptized, they received the ability to go to heaven when they died, and they also received the theological virtues of faith, hope and love. Now, a *virtus* in Latin was an ability to do something good, in contrast to a vice or *vitium*, which was the ability to do something bad. Thus understood, Christian baptism bestowed the ability to have faith in the one true God, it bestowed the virtue of hope or the ability to long for heaven instead of seeing death as the ultimate end, and it bestowed the virtue of charity or the ability to love as Christ loved.

When Christians were confirmed, they received the gifts of the Holy Spirit, which were understood to be wisdom, understanding, counsel, knowledge, fortitude, piety, and fear of the Lord. In other words, they received these spiritual abilities to a more than natural degree, and in this sense they were supernatural abilities.

When men were ordained, as we have already seen, they received priestly powers that enabled them to do things that the laity could not do.

When a man and woman were married, they received the ability to have sexual relations without committing sin, to have legitimate offspring, and to remain married forever.

When a man was ordained, as we have already seen, he received the power to forgive sins and to confect the Eucharist. In the medieval understanding of ordination, priests also received the ability to administer confirmation and to ordain priests, but these powers were reserved to bishops in the medieval church, and so they could not licitly be exercised by priests. Being elevated to the order of bishop did not bestow any additional priestly powers, therefore. It gave only administrative jurisdiction, which was not regarded as a supernatural power.

When a person confessed sins to a priest and received the sacrament of penance, it was not clear what supernatural abilities were received. Some proposed that it was the gift of perfect contrition, to be sorry for having offended God and not merely out of fear of punishment. Others speculated that it was a greater than normal power to avoid sinning in the future.

The same uncertainty hung over extreme unction, the last anointing. In the absence of information from people who had received the sacrament just before dying, it was hard to specify what the effects were, beyond the ability to have a happy death.

*

The Eucharist was a special case.

As we have already seen, it was the special status of the Eucharist that provided a clue to the existence of the *sacramentum et res* or sacramental reality in the other sacraments. Nonetheless, explaining how the bread and wine changed into the body and blood of Christ provided the schoolmen with a unique challenge.

Aristotle had recognized two kinds of change in the world. The most frequent kind was technically called accidental change, a change in the appearance or sensible qualities (*accidentalia*) of things. Changes in size, shape, color, smell, taste or location were all considered changes in the *accidentalia* belonging to things. But there are also times when things change into something completely different. When wood burns, it becomes ashes, for example, and when a person dies, a human being becomes a corpse. The technical name for this was substantial change, for in the scholastic philosophical vocabulary, a *substantia* was an individual thing. Aristotle would have considered the change of a seed into a plant or a caterpillar into a butterfly as instances of substantial change, which modern biology would not do, because as far as he could see, one thing changed into another thing.

From these examples, it is clear that whenever there was a change from one thing into another thing, its accidents or sensible qualities also changed. Christians believed, however, that bread and wine were changed into the body and blood of Christ, yet after this change occurred, there was no change in appearance. The consecrated bread and wine looked and tasted just like the unconsecrated bread and wine.

Schoolmen proposed a number of theories to explain this special sort of change. According to some, when a priest spoke the words of consecration at mass, God replaced the bread and wine with the body and blood of Christ while allowing their appearance to remain the same. This theory of substitution, as it was called, was rejected on the theological grounds that the church's belief was that the bread and wine are changed into the body and blood of Christ, and replacement or substitution was not truly change.

According to others, God adds the body and blood of Christ to the bread and wine, again without the appearances changing. The proponents of this theory appealed to the fathers of the church, some of whom referred to the Eucharist as bread and wine while acknowledging it as the body and blood of Christ. This theory was called consubstantiation from the prefix *con* meaning with, combined with the noun *substantia*. Its opponents argued that it had the same shortcoming as the substitution theory because it claimed that the bread and wine did not truly change; instead, the body and blood of Christ were added to them. Moreover, it had the drawback of claiming that two individual things could exist under the appearances of one of them, which was not very Aristotelian. Nevertheless, consubstantiation remained a popular explanation of eucharistic change until the sixteenth century. It explained why devout Christians could look upon the consecrated elements and perceive bread and wine in one moment and the presence of Christ in the next.

This is a good place to step back and ask what the schoolmen were trying to explain. Were they trying to explain a religious belief, a religious experience, or both? I would suggest that, being the scientists that they were, they were trying to explain both. They believed in the change because they were Christians, and they tried to explain it because they experienced it.

The experience of divine presence is not uncommon in traditional cultures, even if it is becoming increasingly rare in our secular society. Mystics and poets in the past have written about experiencing God, and even today people who are religiously devout (Christians as well as others) will sometimes talk about feeling the presence of God. And although the language of psychology did not exist in the ancient and medieval worlds, Christian intellectuals in both eras sometimes wrote in ways that suggest that they were referring not simply to religious beliefs but also to religious experiences.

The medieval schoolmen were almost all priests. Moreover, it was customary at the time for priests to say mass once a day even if they had to do it alone, without anyone else in attendance. Under the influence of Cyril of Jerusalem, whose text on the eucharistic liturgy was included in the medieval text books, the mass had come to be regarded as a participation in the sacrifice of Christ on the cross, and priests were encouraged to offer the sacrifice of the mass every day because of the spiritual benefits wrought by Christ's sacrifice.

Under such circumstances, it is quite plausible that devout priests who were also theologians had experiences of divine presence while saying the mass. Before they said the words of consecration, they could look at the bread and wine and perceive bread and wine, but after they said the words of consecration, they could look at the objects on the altar in front of them and perceive the presence of Christ. If you are an older Catholic who remembers having experiences like this when you were younger, of if you are a religiously devout Catholic of any age, you know what I am talking about. Even today, when people worship Christ in the Eucharist, either at mass or during Exposition of the Blessed Sacrament, they experience what they can honestly call the real presence of Christ.

Presumably, then, the schoolmen who proposed theories about how bread and wine changed into the body and blood of Christ knew what they were talking about. That is, they knew from personal experience that a change happened before their very eyes. They were not simply exegetes interpreting the words of a doctrine, nor were they apologists explaining a ritual for the benefit of those who had never participated in it. Rather, they were scientists, and as scientists, they would have known what they were talking about. It was something they had personally experienced, but Aristotle's theories of accidental and substantial change could not explain how this change occurred. Hence the need for a new theory to explain it.

The third theory is the one that Thomas Aquinas and the other more astute Aristotelians subscribed to. According to the theory of transubstantiation (*trans* in Latin meaning across, or from–to), consecration of the eucharistic elements caused a genuine change from bread and wine into the body and blood of Christ. This change from one reality into another reality was, in Aristotelian terms, a substantial change, and it was something they could verify from their own experience. At the same time, the accidents of the bread and wine did not change, which they could also verify from their own experience. Therefore, the change from bread and wine to the body and blood of Christ was not a substantial change in the traditional sense of that term. And so this genuine change, a change in reality that did not entail a change in appearances had to be called something else, namely, a transubstantial change.

*

The mass was not a sacrament but a sacrifice.

All the other sacraments are rituals or ceremonies, but the Eucharist is not. To some extent, this is the result of Peter Lombard listing it with six other church rituals. To a greater extent, however, Lombard had no choice since the bread and wine used in the liturgy had been called a sacrament since patristic times.

Earlier in the Middle Ages, some bishops and monks had tried to explain the mass to people as an allegory of the life of Christ. They suggested, for example, that the opening prayers were like the prophets announcing the coming of Christ, the singing of the Gloria represented the singing of the angels when Christ was born, the reading of a passage from the gospels was analogous to the preaching of Jesus during his public ministry, the separate consecration of the bread and wine symbolized Christ's death, and dropping a piece of the host into the chalice afterwards represented his resurrection through the reuniting of his body and hid blood.

As writings of the church fathers got collected into text books, there were some that talked about the eucharistic liturgy as a sacrifice, not in a metaphorical sense, but as a metaphysical reality. By the twelfth century, then, it was generally agreed that the mass was truly a sacrifice. Many prayers in the mass indicated as such, so the challenge to the schoolmen was to find a scientific explanation of how the sacrifice occurred and what effects it had.

The solution came in the form of a philosophical idea from Plato rather than Aristotle. Plato had been Aristotle's teacher in fourth century BC Greece, and many Christian thinkers during the patristic era were more familiar with the writings of Plato and his disciples than they were with the more scientific works of Aristotle. Plato theorized that the reason two objects could be called by the same name (for example, two swords or two horses) was that there existed in a metaphysical realm the ideal archetype in which they both participated. Thus every sword participated in the metaphysical archetype, for example, and when anyone looked at a sword, their eyes saw a physical object but their mind perceived the model that existed in the realm of ideas.

Once the eucharistic liturgy was called a sacrifice, it was easy to interpret it along Platonic lines. If the mass was a sacrifice, then it participated in the heavenly sacrifice described in the Epistle to the Hebrews. Just as Christ, the victim on the cross, offered himself to God the Father in atonement for sins, so also Christ under the appearances of bread and wine was offered to God in atonement for sins. The Latin word for a sacrificial victim was *hostia*, so the bread used in the sacrifice of the mass was called a host. Through participation in the divine reality, the sacrifice of the mass made the sacrifice of Christ present in space and time. The mass did not represent Christ's sacrificial death but it actually re-presented it on earth, that is, the mass made the once-and-for-all sacrifice of Christ present in many places and times so that Christians could enter that eternal moment and experience its spiritual benefits.

Moreover, since the priest at mass offered the consecrated elements to God the Father, the priest participated in the priesthood of Christ as offering himself eternally in heaven. Thus the Catholic priest came to be seen as another Christ (*alter Christus* in Latin), as one having supernatural powers that participated in the divinity of Christ himself, especially the power to offer the sacrifice of the mass and the power to forgive sins.

In this way, the mass as a metaphysical sacrifice was given a metaphysical explanation.

*

The metaphysical theology of the sacraments, developed by the schoolmen in the Middle Ages, became Catholic doctrine centuries later, at the Council of Trent.

During the centuries that followed the high point of medieval scholasticism, changes in the church and changes in the world led to questioning of the scholastic achievement. Christians continued to believe that the mass and the sacraments had metaphysical effects, but increasingly the sacraments became objects of magical thinking. Infants were baptized shortly after birth to prevent their souls from going to hell if they died without the sacrament. Confirmation did not seem to provide any observable benefits, so it continued to be widely neglected. Fear kept many from receiving the Eucharist, for they regarded themselves as too sinful to be touched by God directly, so the hierarchy mandated the reception of communion at least once a year at Easter time. At the same time, reverence for the body of Christ devolved into superstitions such as gazing on the host elevated at mass for good luck.

The sacrament of penance too was believed to wipe sins off one's soul provided that it was done in the right way. This too was an example of magical thinking, as when spells need to be pronounced correctly in order to be effective. Likewise, extreme unction or the last anointing, if done correctly, was hoped to guarantee entrance into heaven.

The problem with metaphysical explanations is that they lead to magical thinking, and magical thinking is uncritical, that is, it is unable to question or correct itself. Thus, when the Middle Ages blended into the Renaissance and the rise of modern science, educated Christians such as Martin Luther began to cast a critical eye on what they perceived as superstitious religiosity. Since the bishops and the pope benefited from the people's superstitions, however, such as charging money for the forgiveness of sins and selling church offices, the hierarchy was not inclined to question the system.

Not until the Catholic Church lost much of Europe to the Protestants was the Catholic hierarchy motivated to action. Bishops assembled in the mid-sixteenth century for the Council of Trent, which met for the dual purpose of rebutting the Protestants and putting the Catholic house in order. The popes who convened the council and those who came after it succeeded in eliminating the most egregious abuses, but in doing so they reaffirmed the metaphysical interpretation of the sacraments. Indeed, they could do nothing else, since the metaphors behind the metaphysics were lost in history.

What came to be called Tridentine Catholicism, which lasted from the Council of Trent to the Second Vatican Council, was a religion of metaphysical beliefs (as most religions are) and strict rules. The rules did not prevent the pope and bishops from meddling in politics, nor did it prevent priests from sexually abusing women and children, nor did it prevent the laity from engaging in magical thinking, but they did maintain a credible religious institution for millions of Catholics for centuries.

4

Religion and Reality

WITHOUT RELIGION, WE WOULDN'T be here today.

In chapter 1, I pointed out that in pre-literate or non-writing cultures, information is stored and retrieved in myths and rituals. Myths are stories in which people can locate themselves in time and space. They are sacred or precious because they tell us basic and important things about ourselves. They tell us who we are and where we came from. In doing so, myths give us a sense of identity and purpose. Rituals are actions or sets of actions that are repeated in the same way every time they are performed. They make life easier because, once we have learned to do something, we do not have to learn to do it again. Rituals are learned habits that save time and help us to live better.

White Americans grow up learning the stories of the Pilgrims landing on Plymouth Rock and celebrating the first Thanksgiving, we learn the stories of the American Revolution, the Declaration of Independence, the early pioneers heading west in wagon trains, the Civil War, and the American contribution to winning the two world wars. These are myths in the technical sense of being stories that give us a sense of identity as Americans. Even if our grandparents or parents were immigrants, we adopt the American mythology as our own, taking the American way of life for granted and pursuing the American dream.

The most basic rituals are what today we would call routines. When we are very young, our parents teach us how to use the potty, and once we have learned it, we keep doing it. Dressing is another routine: underwear and socks first, then clothes and shoes on top of them, and not the other way around. We had to be taught to tie our own shoes, but once we have mastered that complex activity, we do it rather ritualistically. The patterns of our daily lives, getting up in the morning and going to bed at night, tend to settle into routines as we get older. The same can be said of the route we travel to and from work, and even of what we do at work every day. Our lives are filled with routines that were once rituals that we had to learn and that, very often, someone had to teach us.

Name some rituals you had to learn, but which have since become routine? Who taught you those rituals? If no one taught you, why did you decide to learn them?

*

Did religion have a beginning?

In the nineteenth century, anthropologists traveled into unexplored areas of Africa in an attempt to investigate the origins of religion among the tribal peoples of the jungle and the savannah. When Europeans first encountered pygmies in central Africa, so the story goes, they thought they had found a group of human beings who had no religion whatever. They seemed to have no religious festivals, no priests or religious leaders, and they worshiped no identifiable gods. After they began to learn the native language, however, the anthropologists came to the realization that pygmies simply did not differentiate the secular from the sacred. To them, all was sacred. In a sense, they lived their religion from morning to night.

The word "religion" comes from the Latin root *lig*, meaning to connect, and the prefix *re*, meaning again. The root *lig* is found in the word "ligament," which in animals connects muscles to bones. The prefix *re* is found in words like "retell," "relive" and "rethink." It means to do those things again. So the root meaning of the word "religion" is to reconnect.

The pygmies and other tribal peoples connect and reconnect with who they are, where they come from, and how to behave as adult men and women by listening to stories about imaginary or real beings and by repeating actions in the stories that they are told to emulate—stories of bravery and honesty, of fidelity and loyalty, of obedience and self-sacrifice, or cleverness and persistence. Boys learn to hunt from listening to stories of the hunt long before they can carry a spear. Girls learn to gather from listening to stories about what to pick and what to avoid, about the medicinal qualities of some plants, and about women who saved others by using the skills they had learned as girls.

Our pre-human ancestors discovered how to turn stones into tools, and they passed that knowledge from one generation to the next in rituals that turned into routines. They discovered how to turn animal skins into clothing, and they passed that knowledge along in the same way. Hunting, food preparation, building shelter, raising children and a host of other routine activities were learned, remembered and passed on to the next generation through learned rituals and, when language developed, through stories.

Early rituals and myths were precious in the sense that they preserved and enhanced life, they made the lives of early humans somewhat better than the lives of animals, and they gave a basic sense of order to their existence. We can appreciate why they would want to connect and reconnect with what was collectively understood by the tribe or clan. Such knowledge was sacred in the sense that it was crucial to their way of life, and even to their staying alive. The preservation and transmission of such knowledge was the earliest form of religion, the earliest way that humans connected and reconnected with precious information.

In this sense, then, religion made cultural evolution possible.

*

Imagine living in a tribal society, long before the invention of farming.

Farming, or the systematic cultivation of certain plants, began about ten thousand years ago in what today we call the Middle East. Before then, all humans lived in family groups or clans, or in larger groups called bands or tribes.

Tribes are hunter-gatherers. Generally, the men are the hunters, and while they are looking for animals that can be eaten, the women stay behind with the children, looking around for plants and berries that can be eaten. This pattern is repeated even today. Generally, men go to a store looking to buy something, and when they have found it, they bring it home. When women go shopping, on the other hand, they often browse around, looking for things that might be useful or attractive.

Very often, hunter-gatherers are not sedentary. They have to go where the food is. In the northern hemisphere, tribes often migrated south in the winter and north in the summer, following the migration of herd animals and looking for grasses, seeds and berries as they ripen in the spring, and for fruits and nuts as they become available in the summer and fall.

Tribal peoples living in warmer climates, such as the tropics, did not have to migrate. Their food supply was fairly constant. Also, hunter-gatherers in the tropics did not need much in the way of clothing, since the temperature was warm to hot all year.

Tribal culture, as you might imagine, is rather egalitarian. No one amasses great wealth, not only because there is little to amass, but also because one's belongings have to be carried whenever the tribe moves to a different place. Migrating tribes did not have pack animals such as horses, which were domesticated only after the invention of farming.

Tribal life is egalitarian for other reasons as well. If the group is living literally from hand to mouth (there being no way to store food except nuts and seeds) everyone is needed to contribute to the food supply. In addition to hunters and gatherers, there may be a minimal division of labor into tool makers, food preparers, clothing makers, and so on, but many individuals would have a variety of skills, and elaborate tasks such as building shelters would require many hands. Art, too, has its primitive beginnings in tribal culture.

As already mentioned, communal knowledge in societies before the invention of writing is preserved and passed from generation to generation in myths and rituals. With plenty of time for story telling and listening, myths could be repeated until everyone knew them, understanding who they were, what the world was like, and how they should behave. Practical rituals such as food preparation or tool making could be repeated until the young had mastered the skills being taught by their elders. The life of the tribe depended literally on the young learning the myths and rituals taught by their elders.

*

Not all rituals involved practical knowledge, however.

Fairly early in human cultural evolution, people learned to express feelings in ritual. Perhaps it would be the celebration of a successful hunt while the food was being prepared. Perhaps it would be the mourning of a death, for death was plentiful when the average life expectancy was thirty or forty years. Perhaps it would be the sharing of joy at the birth of a child. Perhaps it would be when winter gave way to spring, or spring gave way to summer, rejoicing that the stories predicting such changes in the seasons were indeed true.

Such rituals do not make anything happen. Rather, they celebrate what has happened and what is happening, intensifying the participants' awareness of and appreciation for meaningful events. Rituals of this sort still occur in our society today. Sports teams celebrate victories, and families mourn losses. Some celebrations are repeated on a yearly basis, like birthdays and anniversaries and national holidays.

What are some rituals of this sort that you can think of? Can you identify some of the repeated ritual elements in each of the celebrations?

Other rituals, however, do make something happen. Two people go through a wedding ceremony and they become a married couple. Foreigners go through a naturalization ceremony and become citizens. Citizens who win elections go through an inauguration ceremony and become public officials. Such rituals are not new. They go back to when people were living in tribal cultures. Individuals were joined in wedlock through rituals that might seem strange to us, but they were rituals nonetheless. Any trading that took place between individuals or between groups was done according to established rituals. We do the same, whether the ritual involves handing over cash or signing a credit card receipt.

Rituals of this second sort are called transition rituals or rites of passage. People who go through them have a different status in society after the ceremony. Married people are different from singles, citizens are different from foreigners, public officials are different from ordinary citizens, and so on. Organizations that are hierarchical in nature, such as the military, use ceremonies to facilitate and publicize the transition from lower to higher ranks.

You have probably been through or witnessed a number of transition rituals. Can you name some of them?

*

Transition rituals work without people understanding how they work.

When someone becomes the president of a country, or the governor of a state, or the mayor of a city, or a chief of police, how does that happen? The person looks the same as he or she did before the swearing-in ceremony, but something about them has really changed. Suddenly they are different. Mr. Citizen has become Mr. President. Mrs. Citizen has become

Madam Governor. Officer So-and-so had become Chief So-and-so. Very often, after the ceremony they have powers that they did not have before. The person who becomes president suddenly becomes commander-in-chief of the armed forces. The person who becomes governor can now sign or veto bills passed by the legislature. Where and how do they get that power?

Most people do not know, and most people do not care. It is something that they take for granted. It is something that happens often in their social experience, so they do not think about it.

The schoolmen in the Middle Ages were different. They were curious. They had a scientific mentality. And they had the scientific works of Aristotle, especially his books on physics and metaphysics, to help them understand what was going on in their world.

According to Aristotelian theory, change does not occur without a cause. This is a fairly commonsense observation with regard to the natural world, which is what Aristotle had in mind when he formulated his theory of change. What causes objects to move and to stop moving? Why do rocks fall, and why does smoke rise? What are things made of? What is their nature? How do living things come into existence? What happens to living things when they die? What can be learned about the world around us through observation and logic?

The schoolmen at the University of Paris, however, wanted to use Aristotle's theory of causation to understand changes in people, in particular the changes that occur when people participate in sacramental rituals. A baby who is baptized becomes a Christian and is filled with grace. A woman who goes to confession has her sins forgiven. A man who is ordained receives priestly powers. A couple who are married become husband and wife. The words of consecration turn bread and wine into the body and blood of Christ. How do these changes occur? Is there a theory that can explain them? If so, then the theory would be a theological one, a sacramental theology.

In the previous chapter, we saw how the schoolmen developed scholastic sacramental theology. In this chapter, two things need to be pointed out. The first is that in using Aristotle's theory of change, they adapted a theory about change in the natural world to change in the social world—how baptism changes pagans into Christians, how ordination changes laymen into priests, and so on—which is something the original theory was never meant to do. The fact that the schoolmen had to introduce new concepts in order to explain eucharistic change is further evidence that Aristotle's ideas

75

about natural change were inadequate for explaining what the schoolmen took to be supernatural changes.

The second thing to notice here is that the schoolmen were using Aristotelian theory to explain the Christian myth as it was lived in the Middle Ages. One aspect of the myth was the assumption that the stories in the Bible are factual accounts and so the words of scripture could be taken at face value. Today we would call this interpreting the Bible literally rather than critically. Another aspect of the medieval myth was that there was a direct connection between Christian rituals in twelfth-century Europe and those of first-century Palestine. In other words, infant baptism was essentially the same as the adult baptisms described in the Act of the Apostles, the mass was essentially the same as the Last Supper, extreme unction was essentially the same as the anointing of the sick in the Epistle of James, and so on. Most historians today do not make these assumptions.

*

Myth and ritual, although extremely important, are not self-critical.

Being self-critical means being able to take a step back (metaphorically, of course) and take a look at (another metaphor) what we think, what we say, or what we do. In less metaphorical terms, it means thinking about ourselves and asking questions about our thoughts, words or actions. Was that the right thing to say? Could my words have been taken the wrong way? Why was she offended after I did that? What can I learn from having made that mistake?

What are some times that you have been self-critical? What were you criticizing yourself for?

It is easier to be self-critical about things that we have said or done than it is to be self-critical about what we think. In our minds, the memories of our words and actions live in the past tense, so to speak. I said this to him yesterday. I used to do that. Thoughts and ways of thinking, however, become habitual, they are with us all the time, and they sink into the background of our minds. They remain somewhat subconscious until we need them to understand something, or interpret something, or respond to something. They are, in a sense, ideas that are lying in wait until we need to use them.

Since the ideas that we have internalized are the things that we use to think about ourselves and about what is going on around us, it is difficult to be self-critical about them. A good example of this is a prejudice.

Say, for example, that you think that poor people are lazy and therefore responsible for their own poverty. If this is the case, then it is difficult to see or hear about a poor person without that thought coming into your mind and coloring your perception of that person. You may believe that it would be impolite to say what you are thinking out loud (another example of an internalized thought) and so you smile and interact with the person without revealing your true feelings.

Other examples of prejudices include the following. Abortion providers are going to hell. Conservatives are closed-minded. Liberals believe nothing is immoral. Muslims approve of terrorism. Catholics are credulous. Fat people are slobs. Jews hate Palestinians. Rich people don't care about the rest of us.

What are some prejudices you have perceived in others? What are some of your own prejudices? What do you think about those prejudices?

If you can answer the last two questions, then you are able to be self-critical. If not, this may be something that you should work on.

*

It is hard to be self-critical about our own myths.

Myths are like prejudices in the sense that they contain sets of judgments that we have accepted about the world in which we live. If a prejudice is a pre-judgment about something, a myth is a collection of pre-judgments or already-believed ideas about the world in which we live. It is a set of preconceptions that give us a sense of who we are and what our place in the world is. As was noticed at the beginning of this chapter, those of us who are white Americans believe a collection of stories about white people discovering, colonizing, building, and fighting for the land that became the United States. This is the American myth—a myth in the technical sense of being an indefinite set of ideas that give us a sense of who we are, where we came from, and where we are going as Americans.

What is your conception of the American myth? Articulate it, if you can, especially if it is different from the summary in the paragraph above.

If you are not a white person in the United States or an immigrant who has adopted the American myth, what is the mythic narrative within which you situate yourself and which you use to interpret what you see happening in American society?

People in other countries live within their own national myths just as surely as they live within certain geographical boundaries. Whether they are Europeans or Asians or Africans or Latin Americans, they all carry conceptions about who they are, their way of life, their customs and their values. Myths are not bounded by geography, however. We carry our myths with us even when we travel abroad. What is sometimes called "the ugly American" is someone who travels in foreign countries while thinking that American culture is superior to all others and belittling other people's way of life. It is as though they cannot get out of the American myth in order to understand and appreciate the cultural myths and customs of others.

Living in one myth does not exclude living in others. People with a strong ethnic heritage think of themselves not only as Americans but also as Irish or Italian or Polish or Black or Mexican or Chinese or whatever. People with a strong regional identity think of themselves as Southerners, New Englanders, Californians, Texans or Minnesotans. People from large cites think of themselves as New Yorkers, Chicagoans, Angelinos, or New Orleaneans. People with a strong occupational identity think of themselves as farmers, ranchers, professionals, middle class, students, or retired. We wear many hats, we live in many communities, we belong to many groups, and each one provides us with a vague or vivid myth with which we can identify and which gives us a sense of identity.

What are some mythic ideas or stories about ethnic groups that you belong to? About your family of origin? About the kind of work you do? About the part of the country where you live? Very often these are ideas that we take for granted about ourselves.

*

Religious people also have myths. Better put, myths have them.

Not very long ago, scholars who suggested that the Bible contains myths were roundly condemned. In ordinary language, the word "myth" is taken to be the opposite of the word "truth." If we believe something is not true, we might say, "That's just a myth."

The word "myth" comes from the Greek word *mythos*, which means a story, in contrast with *historia*, which means a factual story. We tend to think of myths as stories that are not true, and of history as stories that are true. To the ancient Greeks, however, *historia* told of things there were true once, such as when a person was born, or the city in which he lived. *Mythos*, on the other hand, told of things that were always true, like tales of courage and cowardice, of love and betrayal, of fidelity and foolhardiness. Think of the Greek and Roman gods and goddesses you may have learned about in classes about literature or art history. Think of Homer's *Iliad* and *Odyssey*, and of the virtues and vices illustrated by Helen and Paris, Agamemnon and Menelaus, Hector and Achilles. These stories, like any classic fiction, are more about spiritual realities than about particular events.

In the twentieth century, anthropologists and religion scholars began to use the word "myth" in the sense of *mythos*, that is, a story about things that are always true—about what is known of the universe, about natural phenomena, about the right and wrong ways to behave, and even about how to do things such as hunting, planting, or building a hut. As already suggested, myth is uncritical, but in a world where knowledge is scarce, even uncritical knowledge is better than ignorance.

In this sense, the two creation stories at the beginning of the Bible are myths. If they were *historia*, they would be contradictory because they give two very different accounts of how the world came into existence and how human beings were first created. But since they are *mythos*, Jews and Christians for centuries could listen to them and find things to learn from each of them. Not noticing that the two creation accounts are factually in-compatible is a good example of how mythic thinking is uncritical.

The same can be said of the two infancy narratives in the New Testa-ment. Matthew tells a story in which God's messenger (*angelos* in Greek means messenger, not angel) speaks to Joseph in Bethlehem, telling him to marry the pregnant Mary, then telling him to flee to Egypt, then telling him to return after King Herod has died. In Matthew's story, Jesus is born in Bethlehem but is taken to live in Nazareth when the family returns to Palestine. Luke tells a story in which God's messenger speaks to Mary who is living in Nazareth, but who has to travel to Bethlehem with her hus-band Joseph to be counted in a Roman census. While they are there, Jesus is born, and the family returns to Nazareth, where Jesus grows up. Luke's story is very different from Matthew's.

As *historia*, the two accounts are incompatible; they cannot both be factually accurate. But as *mythos*, both accounts convey the understanding that Jesus is special, that he was born in Bethlehem (where the messiah was expected to be born), and that he grew up in Nazareth. Christmas pageants, even today, display the uncritical nature of mythic thinking by weaving elements of both stories into a single narrative.

Scripture scholars debate how much of the gospels is *historia* and how much is *mythos*, but those debates miss the point that devout Christians accept the stories as always true, as stories from which they learn the right way to live—to be obedient to God, to be merciful and just, to love God above all and to love one's neighbor as oneself, to give to Caesar what belongs to Caesar and to give to God what belongs to God. They also learn to have faith in Christ and to believe even though they have not seen, to forgive one another, to love their enemies, to minister to the needs of others, and to hope for resurrection on the last day.

People who live deeply within the Christian myth are surrounded by the stories and teachings that they have heard, thought about and meditated on over and over. The Jesus myth becomes inseparable from the way they think about themselves. But the Christian myth goes beyond the gospels to include the rest of the New Testament, for example, the communalism and evangelism of the Book of Acts, the high christology of the fourth gospel and some of the epistles, and the apocalyptic imagery of the Book of Revelation. By living within it, the Christian myth gives devout believers meaning and purpose and direction.

Anyone who is familiar with the story of Francis of Assisi knows that he read only the Gospel According to Matthew, but he internalized it and lived it in such a radical way that he attracted followers without wanting to. Similarly, Mother Teresa of Calcutta followed Christ's call to compassion and ministry in such a way that her life attracted followers the way Jesus' life had attracted followers. Moreover, Catholics are not the only ones whose lives have been deeply immersed in the Christian myth. The names Dietrich Bonhoeffer and Martin Luther King come to my mind. Are there other names that come to your mind?

Nevertheless, mythic thinking remains uncritical. In the past, Protestants and Catholics denounced each other as heretics and swore the other was going to hell. Today the division tends to be between liberals and conservatives of whatever churches, and even within the churches themselves. The uncritical nature of mythic thinking helps explain why religious people are sometimes incapable of examining their own beliefs and values.

*

Mythic thinking is related to magical thinking.

Mythic thinking is completely natural. We all live in a thought world full of assumptions that we do not critically examine. Generally speaking, it takes a jarring personal experience to get us to think about something we take for granted about people, about money, about race, about religion, about politics, or whatever. Encountering counter-factual evidence and admitting it into our consciousness (instead of closing our mind to it) creates what psychologists call cognitive dissonance. We experience something that does not agree with our beliefs. In order to resolve the mental tension, we need to either deny the experience or change our beliefs.

I remember listening to a man recalling that when he was a boy, he was taught that Jews were dishonest and stingy. When he became a teenager, however, he went to work for a Jewish shopkeeper who was meticulously honest with his customers, and who was very generous to his employees. Working through the feelings of cognitive dissonance that bothered him for a while, he finally decided to let go of his prejudice and to take personal experience as a better source of information about Jewish people.

Have you ever experienced cognitive dissonance of this sort? If so, how did you resolve it?

Magical thinking is just as natural. In fact, it is one of the first ways we learn to think, and it never leaves us. What I am calling magical thinking is grasping the connection between two events, a cause and an effect, without understanding how the cause produces the effect.

One definition of a baby is a long tube with a loud noise at one end and no sense of responsibility at the other. As newborns, we experience discomfort of some sort, and we spontaneously cry. Then we are given something to suck on, or we are dried off and held, and the crying stops. At some point, we put two and two together, so to speak, and cry when we want attention. We recognize cause and effect.

Some months later, when we have developed some strength in our muscles, we might be lying on our back in a crib that has some colored objects strung across our line of vision. Perhaps our parents have heard that having something to look up at will help us develop the muscles in our eyes. At a certain point, we arch our back and then relax. The colored objects move for a while, and then they stop. Later, we arch our back again and then relax. Once again the objects move. Dimly we sense a connection between what we are doing and what the objects are doing. We repeat what we are doing and notice one again that the colored shapes move right away.

Another perception of cause and effect. Notice that we do not have to understand why what we do makes something happen. It just happens—like magic.

Magical thinking is the simplest form of cognition. Even animals do it. Pavlov proved this when he trained a dog to salivate when a bell was rung. But pets learn things like this on their own. You take out a leash and your dog gets all excited about going for a walk. You come home after work, and your cats head for the food dish.

We never forget how to do this simple form of causal thinking. In fact we do it all the time. We enter a dark room, turn up a wall switch, and the lights come on. Cause and effect. We knew what would happen. In fact, we would be quite surprised if the lights did not come on. Moreover, we can perform this simple operation without any comprehension of electricity, wiring, or building construction. We just have to know that if we turn up a switch, the lights come on.

We use magical thinking in all of our interactions with technology. We turn the key in the ignition switch (or, in later model cars, we press the start button), and the engine comes on. We hit the keys on the computer keyboard or on the smart phone, and letters appear on the screen in front of our eyes—like magic! We have no idea how what we are doing causes the effect we perceive, nor do we need to in order to drive a car or use a computer. But when our action does not produce the desired effect—when the car does not run or the computer does not work—we are helpless to make any repairs. We need to take the machine to someone who actually understands the relationship between what we are doing and what the machine does.

✶

We use magical thinking when we perceive changes produced by rituals.

We spoke above about changes that are produced by rituals, and about how the schoolmen used Aristotelian science to understand how the rituals produced their effects. We can now say that, from a psychological perspective, people in the Middle Ages were using magical thinking when they thought about the sacraments. The changes they perceived were genuine changes, just as truly as the changes we perceive resulting from rituals are genuine changes. People go though a wedding ceremony and they are no longer single, people are inducted into military service and they are no longer civilians. My point is that what the schoolmen explained were real changes.

Today we would not use Aristotelian metaphysics to explain how rituals change people from what they were before the ceremony to what they are after the ceremony. Instead, we might use some form of consent theory. Social consent is involved in what is sometimes called the social construction of reality.

Imagine you are a kid playing hide and seek. Imagine further that you are pretty young, and you have not played this game before. One of the older kids explains the rules to you. One person is It, and the one who is It has to close their eyes and count, say, to 20, while all the others run and hide. After counting, the one who is It goes looking for the ones who are hiding, and tags the first one found. That person now becomes It, everyone comes out of hiding, and the game starts over again.

Typically, a person becomes It by being tagged and hearing the words, "You're It!" This simple ritual changes the social status of the one tagged from someone who is not It to someone who is It. As long as all the kids agree to the rules of the game, one child after another can be It and look for the others who are hiding. Social consent makes the game possible, and consent governs the playing out of the game.

Games, even adult sports, are good examples of social realities that are created by consent. As long as all the players consent to the rules of the game, the game can be played. In a real sense, consent brings the game into existence. Unless all the players consent, the game cannot be played. Even the spectators must consent to the rules of the game if they are to understand the game and appreciate how it is played.

*

People do not think about giving consent to social realities. They just do it.

Part of growing up entails learning the rules of the game of life. More technically, it entails learning the social construct that we call reality. The more tangible aspects of that social construct are human relationships, the web of social connections that enable us to call some people family, others friends, others acquaintances, and so on. At the fringes of that web of relationships are people that we know about but do not necessarily know, for example, store clerks, business owners, school teachers, and government officials. We relate to them, when necessary, through the roles that they play in society. The less tangible aspects of the social construct are what we call culture, which encompasses unwritten rules about how we think about things, what we value, how we relate to other people, what we eat, how we dress, and in general how our society differs from other societies.

In terms of what was discussed in the first chapter, most of the social construct are intangible things or spiritual realities. Relationships, values, principles, rules of etiquette, and social norms are not physical realities, so if they are real at all, they must be spiritual realities. They are ideas and rules that must be learned, so even though we might not consent to them if we had a choice (for example, we might not like how wealth or privileges are distributed in our society), we did tacitly consent, when we were growing up, to learn what it is we needed to know in order to be adults. In this sense, then, we consent to the ways that rituals change people and change interpersonal relationships.

Once we have done this, we do not have to think about how rituals work. We just use magical thinking to perceive them working.

*

Today, in addition to consent theory and psychology, there are additional ways of understanding rituals and how they work.

Early in the twentieth century, psychologists and anthropologists explored the ways that symbols and rituals can trigger religious experiences and then later facilitate encounters with the same experienced realities. Terms such as sacred time, sacred space and sacred meaning were used to describe what people found when they pondered religious texts or meditated without words. Symbols were analyzed in terms of their obvious or surface meaning and the hidden or deeper meaning that they opened up for people who pondered them. Transition rituals or rites of passage were recognized as having three distinct moments: being taken aside or separated from one's usual interactions in society, a marginal or liminal state in which one is neither what one used to be nor what one is going to be, and reintegration in society with a new status or role.

Late in the twentieth century, an entirely new academic discipline emerged. Ritual studies attempted to take what had already been learned about ritual in older social sciences, to systematize it, and to study, sometimes in minute detail, what happened during rituals and what effects they had on individuals and groups. Types of rituals were categorized and classified according to when they occurred, according to why they were used and by whom, according to whether or not they had effects in society, and whether or not they facilitated social processes such as exchange, healing, or the expression of emotions such as joy and grief. Rites were also analyzed according to the degree of formality or informality, the amount of rule governance, the use of symbolism, and dramatic form in terms of having a beginning, climax and denouement.

People who try to understand rituals in the twenty-first century, therefore, do not need to use Aristotelian science to understand rituals and the effect they have on people. Indeed, today in academia it would be quite inappropriate to borrow a theory developed by an ancient Greek philosopher to understand the natural world and use it to understand religious rituals. Yet that is precisely what Catholics do when they talk about the sacraments in terms of matter and form, substance and accidents.

As long as Roman Catholicism retained its medieval cultural form, which is to say until the mid-1960s, the classical Aristotelian analysis used by scholastic theologians seemed to be quite adequate. But this is no longer the case.

*

Something needs to be done.

As noted in the introduction at the beginning of this book, scholastic sacramental theology, based on Aristotelian metaphysics, says that certain things should result from the performance of Catholic sacramental rituals. Babies who are baptized should remain Christians for the rest of their lives. Youngsters who are confirmed should be different from youngsters who are not confirmed. Catholics who morally injure themselves or others should go to a priest to be absolved from their sins. Men who are ordained should be better than people who are not ordained, and they should stay priests for their entire lives. Catholic who marry should never divorce. And people who are sick should ask to be anointed in order to be healed.

But this does not happen any more.

The reason is that medieval ritual theory (a.k.a. scholastic sacramental theology) was based on the personal and social experience of monks who were thinking about Christian life in the Middle Ages. They saw that baptism, confirmation, and ordination were permanent. They saw that marriage lasted until one of the spouses died. They saw that sinners went to confession to be absolved from their sins. They saw that the seriously ill sought to receive extreme unction before they died. And because the monks were devout priests, they said mass every day and experienced the presence of Christ after they consecrated the bread and wine.

It does no good for the Catholic Church to cling to a ritual theory that is based on medieval practices and that relies on Aristotelian science. Catholic experience today is not the same as Catholic experience in the Middle Ages. And no one today uses Greek metaphysics as a basis for ritual theory.

It is time for a fresh start.

5

Ritual and Honesty

One way to define it is thinking on the inside what you are saying on the outside. That is, what you say to yourself is the same as what you say to others.

We all know what this is about. If we think one thing and say another, that's being dishonest. If we know that what we are saying is false, then we are being dishonest.

One stereotype of dishonesty is the used car salesman who says anything to sell a car to an unsuspecting customer. Another is the politician who says anything to get elected. They don't care if what they say corresponds to the facts. They may even be aware that what they are saying is false.

All of us have told lies. We know what it is to tell a lie. We say something that isn't true for one reason or another. At the time, we usually think it's for a good reason.

Let's call this subjective dishonesty. It happens when a person (i.e., a human subject) is aware of saying something that is not true.

But what if a person says something they believe to be true even though it is not true? Someone once asked me to meet her at a certain bus stop, and I said I knew where it was. I waited for her for 30 minutes before driving home without her. She waited for me for 40 minutes at the actual location before calling another friend to drive her home. I thought I was telling the truth, but I wasn't.

I guess we call that a mistake, even an honest mistake. Or we call it an incorrect statement. We say that someone didn't understand the situation, or that they didn't know the facts, or that they didn't realize what they were saying. But we don't accuse them of lying.

*

Is there such a thing as objective dishonesty?

Sure. If someone says something they know to be untrue, then it is objectively the case that they are being subjectively dishonest. The human subject who is telling the falsehood is being dishonest, but looking at it from the outside, as it were, and studying the situation objectively would lead us to say that the person is lying.

If you know for sure that someone is lying, isn't the knowledge of that fact objectively correct? Wouldn't it be objectively true to judge that what is being said is a lie?

*

Can signs and symbols be objectively dishonest?

Since signs and symbols are not self-aware and cannot think for themselves, they cannot be subjectively dishonest. But they can be objectively dishonest if they were created by someone who knew they weren't true, and who posted them anyway, maybe even with the intention of deceiving people.

Let's say someone posts a sign saying that an area is monitored by closed circuit television even though there is no CCTV camera on the premises. Wouldn't that be a lie of sorts? Posting the sign could deter trespassing, and it would be a lot less expensive than installing real security cameras. Hanging a dummy camera on the wall would make the lie more credible, but it would still be a lie.

Or let's say a merchant advertises a 20% off sale but boosts the sticker price by 10% ahead of time in order to deceive shoppers. Another way to do this is to claim that the actual value of a product is higher than it actually is, so shoppers are deceived into thinking they are getting a bargain.

Think of some other ways that signs can be objectively dishonest.

I have said that a sign can be objectively dishonest if someone had been subjectively dishonest in posting something that was known to be untrue. But how should we classify a sign that is misleading even though no one intended it to mislead?

Let's say a road crew misreads the orders they were given, and they post a sign indicating that there is a gas station at a certain exit from the interstate highway. Since there is no gas station at the exit, the sign is misleading because the information it contains is false. Someone who gets off the highway and finds no gas station there might even complain that the sign is deceptive. But we would not call the sign dishonest.

*

The difference between signs and symbols can be a little confusing.

In the examples just given, we were talking about signs that are or contain symbols, but I picked them because they are easy examples to understand.

Both signs and symbols have referents, as discussed in chapter one. But signs in the strictest sense are rather simple, whereas symbols are more complex. Natural signs are easiest to understand. Smoke is a sign of fire, and footprints are a sign that someone has walked by. We might think of green buds on trees as a sign that spring is approaching, and one sign of fall is that the leaves start turning color. In each case, the sign is one thing and what it refers to is something else. Even so, as with symbols, the meaning of a sign is in a human mind, not in the sign itself.

Dirty dishes on the table are a sign that dinner is over, and high school students dressed in evening gowns and tuxedos signals that there is a junior or senior prom nearby. Dust on the shelf indicates that it has not been dusted lately, and the smell of warm bread indicates that bread is baking in the oven.

Can you think of other signs that are not symbols, but just signs?

*

It is easier for symbols to be objectively dishonest, even when no one intends them to be.

Words are symbols, as we saw in chapter one, and in most cases it is hard for words to be objectively dishonest without them also being subjectively dishonest. Here we are not talking about single words but sentences.

It is hard to say something true or false in a single word, but it can be done, as in a one-word answer to a question.

Let us agree, then, that in ordinary speech, it is hard for a sentence to be objectively dishonest without it also being subjectively dishonest. Ordinarily, a sentence is not a lie unless the speaker is intending to deceive by saying something that he or she believes to be false. Can you think of an instance where this is not the case? I can't.

When words get used in rituals, however, it is easy for them to convey something that the speaker does not intend. Someone introduces us to a friend of theirs and we say, "Glad to meet you." In fact, we are not really glad at all (There are exceptions to this.) but we are polite, and so we say, "Glad to meet you," and show that we have good manners.

The same can be said about a handshake. We are introduced to people and we shake their hands, symbolically saying we are glad to meet them, even if we'd rather be somewhere else. In a sense, such handshakes are objectively dishonest even though we are not intending to deceive. We are just trying to be polite.

Moving up the level of emotional intensity, we can consider kissing, which symbolically is an indicator of emotional attraction or attachment. When I was pretty young, I had a girl friend who really liked me. I did not feel toward her the way she felt toward me, but I always kissed her back whenever she kissed me. One reason, of course, is that kissing is enjoyable, even pleasurable, especially when we're young. But another reason is that I did not want to disappoint her, I did not want to make her unhappy. Even though I was trying to be nice to her, I always had a sense that my kisses were somewhat dishonest. I did not want to deceive her, but I knew that I was not being truthful with her.

Can you relate to any of these examples? Can you think of examples of your own?

✳

Can symbols lose their truthfulness over time? I believe this is possible.

In her right hand, the Statue of Liberty carries a torch on high. In her left hand, she holds a tablet with the dates July 4, 1776 (the start of the American Revolution) and July 14, 1789 (the start of the French Revolution). At the entrance to the base of the statue, for all to read, there is a bronze plaque bearing a poem that reads, in part,

Give me your tired, your poor,
Your huddled masses yearning to breathe free,
The wretched refuse of your teeming shore.
Send these, the homeless, tempest-tossed, to me.

The poem accurately reflects the welcoming spirit of the United States around the turn of the twentieth century, which took in millions of immigrants fleeing hunger and political persecution in Europe. For refugees coming by boat into New York harbor, the statue symbolized the promise of freedom and a chance to start a new life.

Not so, today. Whereas European countries have taken in hundreds of thousands of refugees fleeing war in the Middle East and poverty in Africa, the United States admits only a few thousand each year, and this only after careful scrutiny. Some American politicians have even made it a point to denounce immigration and to arouse suspicion about refugees.

It is no longer true to say that America welcomes the tired, the poor, the masses of people yearning to breathe the air of freedom. The plaque with the poem on it is no longer an honest expression of popular sentiment. It is no longer an honest symbol.

*

Sometimes dishonest symbols are recognized and removed.

In recent years, sentiment in the United States has turned against symbols of white supremacy and black oppression. The most prominent of these is the Confederate battle flag, which southern soldiers carried on the field during the Civil War because the South's national flag, the Stars and Bars, was too similar to the North's Stars and Stripes.

In the eighteenth century, after the defeat of the Confederacy, the battle flag was sometimes viewed as a symbol of Southern pride and regional difference, a symbol of being more self-determined than the Yankee North. In the mid-twentieth century, however, as African Americans fought against racial segregation and gained civil rights that had been denied them, the battle flag became viewed by white Southerners who resented social change as a symbol of white supremacy, and by black Southerners who remembered the repression and violence of the Jim Crow days as a symbol of oppression.

In time, this new symbolism became such an irritant to people, black and white, who were sensitive to human rights, that they insisted that the flag be removed from public buildings and parks where it had for decades been legally displayed. The honest symbol of regional difference had become a dishonest symbol of Southern uniqueness when it was used to arouse racial hatred in whites and instill fear and unrest in blacks. Rejection of the flag grew rapidly in the second decade of the twenty-first century, and by 2016 it had disappeared from display on public property.

*

Symbolic honesty and dishonesty are, to some extent, a matter of perception.

When Europeans invaded North and South America, they brought with them symbols of the Christian religion, primarily the cross and the crucifix, and for Catholics, additional symbols such as the statues of saints and the Blessed Sacrament. To European Christians, these were symbols of moral superiority and religious correctness: the Europeans were bringing the true religion and its moral values to benighted savages. To the native Americans, however, these were symbols of conquest and oppression, for the people who professed Christianity lied to the natives, swindled them from their land, robbed and killed them. In Central and South America, the natives were economically and even physically enslaved. In North America, they were marginalized and driven into enclaves called reservations.

We could say that, to the European settlers, symbols of the Christian religion were honest symbols, for they accurately symbolized what they truly believed, or at least what they said they believed. For the native Americans, however, the same symbols were dishonest symbols, for the Christian ministers preached love but the settlers themselves practiced hatred.

Which interpretation of the symbols was correct? They both were, for the Christians perceived the cross as a symbol of salvation, and the native peoples perceived the cross as a symbol of oppression. In the colonial Americas, both spiritual realities were present, and both could be perceived through Christian symbols.

It has been sometimes said that perception is reality; the way we perceive things is the way they are, as far as we are concerned. The technical term for this is one that we have already encountered—the social construction of reality. The real things in question here are not physical realities (mountains, trees, buildings, roads, and so on) but what were called in the first chapter spiritual realities (ideas, values, relationships, societies, and so on).

For this reason, it is often hard to have a conversation with someone with beliefs and values that are different from our own. Spiritual realities are in the background of the thoughts that are in the foreground of our minds. They are the assumptions that shape our perceptions. They are the hidden premises from which we draw our conclusions. Unless and until we can get to the point where we can talk our hidden assumptions and premises, we can never do more than agree to disagree.

In this book, however, I do not want to discuss that deeper issue—which can be a book itself, for it would entail introspection and possibly therapy. I am just trying to help you see how symbols can be both honest and dishonest, that is, they can genuinely symbolize the meanings that gave rise to them, or they can symbolize meanings that are quite different from the original meanings.

Can you come up with your own examples of honest and dishonest symbols—either symbols that changed their meaning over time, or symbols that mean one thing for a certain group and something else to a different group?

*

Symbolic rituals can also be dishonest.

We usually do not think of a handshake as a symbolic ritual. Even so, it is a ritual or patterned set of actions, and it is symbolic because it means something, it has a referent. In this case the referent is a spiritual reality such as acceptance or welcoming. And we have already seen how it can be a dishonest ritual.

Another form of dishonest ritual that is possible in our society is attending a party in honor of someone we do not like, or attending a celebration in which we have no real interest. Sometimes these events are family-related, like going to your aunt's birthday party, not because you like her, but because she might leave you something in her will. Sometimes they are work-related, like an office party that you simply must attend or people will talk. One name for this type of symbolic dishonesty is hypocrisy.

But what if the event itself is hypocritical? What if it is the funeral of a policeman whom you knew was a bad cop? His praises are being sung, but you know he planted evidence to get convictions against innocent people.

What if it is the inauguration of a judge that you know is biased against racial minorities? As a judge, he is supposed to be impartial, but you know that he is anything but impartial in certain types of cases. What if it is a graduation ceremony in a school that basically warehouses children until they are old enough to be pushed out? The ceremony symbolizes success in education, but this is in a school were education does not happen. Wouldn't these be dishonest rituals?

What are some other dishonest rituals you can think of?

*

What, then, is a dishonest ritual?

Thinking about these examples, we can say that a dishonest ritual is one in which the reality being celebrated is not present where the ritual is being performed. An extreme example would be an induction ceremony into a club where the actual objective of a mock ceremony is to ridicule and embarrass the person who thinks she is accepted by the others in the club. A less extreme example would be a Boy Scout being given a merit badge for a skill set that he has not really acquired.

*

Back to religion.

In chapter two, we saw that words originally referring to spiritual realities that were actually experienced were later taken to refer to spiritual realities that are not experienced. I called this second group metaphysical realities, both because the word "metaphysical" means beyond the physical or material world, and because the medieval schoolmen understood them to be metaphysical realities in the sense of that term in Aristotelian science.

A non-traditional examination of some New Testament texts— non-traditional in the sense that it asked questions not usually asked, for example, about experiential referents in the minds of the scriptural authors—revealed the probable referents of a number of terms. These are only probable because, in matters of interpretation, few things can be determined with one hundred percent certainty.

The Greek word *baptisma* originally referred to a visible activity, namely, immersion in water. The word was also used metaphorically to refer to immersion in the Christian community. By Augustine's time, it referred to an invisible sign or mark that was received on the soul of a person undergoing the Christian initiation ritual.

The seal of the spirit, mentioned briefly in two epistles, probably referred to the outward manifestation of inner conversion. Changes in behavior such as virtuous living and engaging in novel activities such as speaking in tongues were regarded as visible evidence that a person had rejected the spirit of this world and had received the spirit of Christ. In the Middle Ages, the rite of confirmation was believed to confer an invisible seal on the soul, which was something quite different from the original referent.

Even the concept of the Holy Spirit, eventually identified as the Third Person of the Blessed Trinity, seems to have originally been a holy spirit, which was a way of naming the source of a person's virtuous or godly behavior. This would have been the opposite of an unclean or evil spirit, which in biblical times was thought to be the source of a person's erratic or immoral behavior.

In ordinary usage, the Greek word for salvation referred to personal welfare or well-being. Therefore, salvation in the New Testament probably referred to being rescued from the moral danger of living in sin, which is to say, living in a way that was harmful to others and ultimately to oneself. Eventually, salvation became identified with going to heaven after dying.

Having faith in Jesus and accepting him as Lord very likely meant trusting that Jesus taught the right way to live, which implied accepting him as one's spiritual master and moral guide. Eventually, faith became purely a matter of belief, that is, believing that Jesus is divine, regardless of how one lived one's life. By the Middle Ages, everyone in Christian Europe believed that Jesus was the Son of God—even liars and adulterers, thieves and murderers.

Although the words for eternal life referred to life after death in some Old Testament passages written originally in Greek rather than in Hebrew, a good case can be made that in many New Testament passages the words refer to a certain quality of life, something like boundless vitality or irrepressible spiritual energy. By the patristic period and certainly by the Middle Ages, however, all references to eternal life were taken to refer to everlasting existence in heaven.

Did those interpretations presented in chapter two make sense to you? Does this summary represent what you got out of reading that chapter? If so, what implications does it have for your understanding of Christianity?

*

The schoolmen in the Middle Ages interpreted the terms just discussed as metaphysical realities, and they explained them using Aristotelian science.

Some of the other terms would have been soul, grace, sacrifice, body of Christ, mystery, sin, absolution, eucharist, priest, marriage, and sacrament.

For interpreting the effects of sacraments on people, the schoolmen borrowed Aristotle's theory of the human soul.

Simply put, rocks and other inanimate things do not have souls. The Latin word for soul is *anima*, which is the root of the word, animate. To the Greek mind, anything that moves or is capable of doing more than a rock does, must have something in it that enables it to do those things. Aristotle called the ability to do something a power.

Thus, plants have the ability to do things that rocks cannot do. They can live, grow, and reproduce. In Aristotelian terminology, plants or vegetative beings have the powers of life, growth, and reproduction. They have vegetative souls.

Next, animals have all the vegetative powers of plants, but they can also see, hear, taste, smell, feel and move about. In Aristotelian terminology, animals have souls with the powers of sight, hearing, taste, smell, touch and local motion.

Lastly, humans have all of the powers of plants and animals, but they can also think, reason, and make decisions. In Aristotelian terminology, humans have souls with the powers of intellect and will.

These powers were understood to be metaphysical in the sense that they were not believed to be based in organs such as the brain or the nervous system. The Greeks did not know much about human anatomy. Rather, the powers were thought of as inhering in the soul—the vegetative soul, the animal soul, or the human soul—and the soul was conceived to be a metaphysical entity. It cannot be experienced, but it is the reason why experience is possible. If the soul leaves the body, so also do its powers, which is why, according to the Greek way of thinking, the dead are not able to do anything.

Now, all of the above-mentioned powers were natural powers or abilities. The schoolmen, however, understood that God gave supernatural powers to Christians. The Latin prefix *super* means above, so a supernatural power in the Middle Ages was thought of as an ability that is above human ability. The clearest example is that of priests. Men who are ordained as priests were thought to have priestly powers—the power to forgive sins, the power to offer the sacrifice of the mass and to confect the Eucharist, the power to prepare the sick for death with extreme unction, and so on— which made them able to do things that ordinary Christians could not do.

How did the schoolmen know this? By observation, of course. They saw priests doing such things and concluded that they had the power to do so. It would be as though a child saw a police officer arresting a man and inferred that the officer had the power to make arrests. We make the same sort of inference when we watch a sidewalk artist making a portrait of a tourist and, as the picture emerges, we realize that the artist has a genuine ability to draw. In other words, the schoolmen knew about priestly powers from their experience in medieval European society.

Christians in the Middle Ages also believed that only Christians were able to get into heaven, that baptism gave them the supernatural virtues of faith, hope and love, that confirmation bestowed the gifts of the Holy Spirit, and that people who married were given the ability to remain married until one of the spouses died. These beliefs were reinforced by the fact that only Christians could be buried in church cemeteries, and by the fact that divorce was impossible in medieval society. The beliefs also justified the forced conversion of pagans and the inhumane treatments of Jews and Muslims who, in the Christian scheme of things, were not blessed by God with any of these special gifts.

Are you beginning to get a feeling for how the Catholic theology of sacraments and the gifts they bestowed on Christians made perfect sense in medieval society?

*

As mentioned in chapter three, the schoolmen were the scientists of their day, but the science that guided their thinking was Aristotelian science. At the risk of repeating myself, let me review some highlights of that chapter in order to focus on ritual honesty in Catholic sacramental practices.

In medieval Europe, there were two primary sources of theological information: experience and the Bible. Experience encompassed social experience, or what society looked like and how people behaved in the Middle Ages, but it also included religious experiences such as the experience of being forgiven after confessing one's sins or the experience of divine presence when praying before the Blessed Sacrament.

A secondary source was writings of early church fathers that had been carefully copied and preserved in monasteries during the Dark Ages that followed the fall of the Roman Empire. Most prominent among the patristic sources were the writings of Tertullian, Cyprian of Carthage, Ambrose of Milan, and Augustine of Hippo, for these fathers had written in Latin, which the schoolmen could easily read. Writings of the Greek fathers, although more numerous, were generally not available in Europe with the exception of excerpts that had been translated into Latin. The schoolmen could not read Greek, and so they even had to use a Latin translation of the Bible.

The primary source of philosophical concepts used by the schoolmen to interpret their personal and social experience on the one hand and biblical passages on the other hand was Aristotelian science. Having lived three centuries before Christ, Aristotle was no Christian, but the schoolmen used his ideas and his method of scientific analysis to develop a systematic understanding of medieval Christian beliefs and practices. I say "medieval" advisedly, because the theology they developed was a reflection on and a reflection of Christian faith during the Middle Ages. They themselves believed that they were uncovering eternal truths, that is, ideas that would remain true forever. They were not aware that their entire enterprise was very culture bound.

We also saw in chapter three that the medieval Christians accepted the notion that there were many *sacramenta* or sacred signs in their religion. Theologians in the universities, however, were primarily interested in those *sacramenta* that were symbolic rituals and that produced effects of some sort. The effects in question were known either through social experience (e.g., pagans became Christians when they were baptized) or through personal experience (e.g., Christ's presence was perceived in the Eucharist). Around 1150, a schoolman named Peter Lombard proposed a list of seven such *sacramenta* that eventually became known as the seven sacraments.

Using Aristotelian science, the schoolmen developed a version of medieval philosophy and theology that is known as scholasticism, which is why the schoolmen themselves are often referred to as scholastic philosophers and theologians. Aristotelian science was an attempt to understand the world by analyzing why things are the way they are. In many respects, it was a very commonsense approach, but it was also fairly systematic.

For example, human artifacts such as a wooden chair can be understood by asking what it is made of (its matter, in this case, wood), what is its shape (its form, in this case, a chair), who made it (the efficient cause, in this case, a carpenter), what was used to make it (the instrumental cause, in this case, woodworking tools), and the purpose for which it was made (the final cause, in this case, to have something to sit on).

Although Aristotle had developed this type of conceptual analysis to understand the natural world, the schoolmen adapted it to understand medieval church rituals. The matter of a sacrament was any material used in the ritual such as water, oil, bread, or wine. The form of the sacrament consisted of the words used in the ritual, such as "I baptize you . . ." or "This is my body . . ." which expressed the essence of the ritual. The efficient cause of the sacrament's effects was understood to be God, for only God could produce supernatural effects such as salvation, the forgiveness of sins, priestly powers, and so on. The instrumental cause of the sacrament's effects was the proper performance of the ritual. (Note that the instrumental cause was not the minister, but what the minister did.) And the final cause was grace, that is, a supernatural gift that was both specific to each sacrament (sacramental grace) and common to all sacraments (sanctifying grace).

The schoolmen made two key adaptations to Aristotelian science so that it could be used to understand how sacraments worked. The first was the introduction of an explanatory concept known in Latin as *sacramentum et res*, literally "sign and thing" or "sacrament and reality," but usually rendered as "sacramental reality" in scholastic theology textbooks. The sacramental reality made it possible for a physical ritual to have metaphysical effects, and it also made it possible for a person who is a natural being to receive supernatural effects.

The second adaptation was an addition to Aristotle's analysis of causality. Aristotle had recognized two categories of change in the natural world. In the first category, the appearance of something changes, for example, leaves turn color in the fall. In the second category, something changes into something else, for example, wood turns into ashes when it is burned. The schoolmen called the first category accidental change because the Latin word for appearances is *accidentalia*. In their terminology, any change in color, size, shape or location was an accidental change. When a baby grows into a child and then into an adult, it goes through a long sequence of accidental changes but it remains the same person through all these changes in its appearance. The schoolmen called the second category substantial change because the Latin word for an individual existing thing is *substantia*. When a human being dies, for example, what remains is no longer a human being but a corpse.

Common to all substantial changes in the natural world is that they always entail accidental changes as well. When a tree dies and becomes wood, it no longer continues to grow and its leaves wither, so its *accidentalia* are different from what they were before. Likewise, when a human being dies and becomes a corpse, it no longer breathes or moves, so its *accidentalia* are different from what they were before.

The schoolmen, however, needed to explain a change from one thing to another even though there was no change in appearances. When bread and wine were consecrated and changed into the body and blood of Christ, their reality changed but there was no change in their appearance. The change in reality was known by faith, but the religiously devout schoolmen also probably knew it by experience. We have to say probably because, with few exceptions, Christians in the Middle Ages did not write about their religious experiences. We do know, however, that it is possible to experience the presence of Christ in the consecrated Eucharist because saints and mystics have written about it, and devout Catholics who grew up before the Second Vatican Council often experienced it.

Have you ever had an experience of God's presence that occurred when you were some place other than in a church? Have you ever experienced the presence of Christ while praying before the Blessed Sacrament, or after receiving holy communion? If you have, then you know what I am talking about.

To explain this type of change, the schoolmen drew upon a concept that we have already discussed, namely, *sacramentum et res* or sacramental reality. In their terminology, when the eucharistic bread and wine were consecrated, a sacramental reality became present under the appearances of bread and wine. This sacramental reality could be affirmed by faith, but it could also be perceived as a sacred or divine presence. Catholics commonly referred to it as the Blessed Sacrament.

In the same way, Catholics have traditionally referred to the sacramental realities received through the other six sacramental rituals as sacraments—the sacrament of baptism, the sacrament of confirmation, the sacrament of penance, and so on. Thus when Catholics talk about receiving the sacraments, what they are talking about is the *sacramentum et res*, or the sacramental reality that, in the scholastic analysis, had to be received in order for supernatural grace to be received into the soul.

*

Sometimes there is no easy explanation for things.

I have presented this rather convoluted account of how the schoolmen used Aristotelian science to understand medieval sacramental beliefs and practices because the simple accounts that Catholics are usually given are misleading. They used to be told (not so much today) that only the baptized can go to heaven, and now we see why: according to scholastic theology, baptism bestowed the supernatural ability needed to behold the Beatific Vision. They are told, even today, that confirmation confers the gifts of the Holy Spirit, and now we see why: according to scholastic theology, every sacrament conferred supernatural gifts of some sort. They are told, even today, that priests have supernatural powers, and now we see why: according to scholastic theology, ordination bestowed priestly powers that lay people do not have. They are told, even today, that marriage is indissoluble, and now we see why: according to scholastic theology, Christians who married received the supernatural grace needed to remain married for the rest of their lives. They are told, even today, that Christ is present in the Blessed Sacrament, and now we see why: according to scholastic theology, priests have the supernatural power to change bread and wine into the body and blood of Christ.

In scholastic terminology, the change from bread and wine into the body and blood of Christ is expressed this way: the substance of the bread and wine are transformed into the substance of Christ's body and blood. (This is where the term, transubstantiation, comes in.) This way of expressing it, however, gives the impression that the stuff called bread and wine are transformed into the stuff of flesh and blood. And this in turn leads to the mistaken belief that Christ is physically present in the Blessed Sacrament.

If Catholics today want to understand the Church's sacramental doctrines, they need to understand where they came from.

*

In the Middle Ages, the Catholic sacraments were honest rituals.

An honest ritual is one in which the reality being celebrated is present where the ritual is being performed. Some simple examples: a baby shower for a woman who is expecting soon, a high school graduation for youngsters who have earned their diploma, a family Thanksgiving dinner that brings brothers and sisters together for a reunion once a year, the nightly opening of a shelter for the homeless, and a company awards banquet for high achievers.

In medieval Europe, the rituals about which the schoolmen wrote were all in existence before the development of scholastic theology. Babies were being baptized, people were going to confession, couples were getting married, young men were being ordained, priests were saying mass every day, and the dying received extreme unction. Of the seven sacraments, only confirmation was haphazardly performed.

During the early Middle Ages, the books that contained sacramental rites had to be copied and recopied. Since the printing press had not yet been invented, all books had to be written by hand every time that a new volume was needed. Books that contained church rituals, of course, were in fairly constant use, in contrast to library books that might be taken off the shelves only occasionally. Students who wanted to read a book often had to make their own copy by hand. The primary way that the works of Aristotle spread through the medieval universities was to have someone read the library copy slowly while a group of students wrote down what they heard.

Although the copying and recopying of ritual books was a laborious process, it also helped keep the sacraments honest. A good example of this is the anointing of the sick. When anointing was first made a church ritual in the ninth century, the prayers asked for the healing of the person being anointed. Over the next few centuries, however, church officials noticed that many of the people who had been anointed did not recover from their illness but, instead, they died. Thus the words of the ritual got changed over the course of time, and by the twelfth century, when it got included in Peter Lombard's list of sacraments, the rite had become a preparation for death named *extrema unctio* or last anointing.

In summary, the words of the rite got changed so that they fit the actual circumstances in which the ritual was used. To put it differently, the words got changed in order to keep the ritual honest.

How were the other sacraments honest?

Ordination is a clear example. Men were ordained into a series of holy orders, and at each stage, the ordained were given new rights and responsibilities. Those in the rank of porter performed practical tasks reserved to clerics. Those ordained as lectors could read before the community. Acolytes were allowed to serve at the altar. Exorcists were permitted to pray for those who asked for a blessing. Subdeacons and deacons were given almost priestly responsibilities during a solemn mass. But only those ordained as priests could offer the holy sacrifice, hear confessions and anoint the sick. Each of the rites said what it did, and each of the ceremonies effected changes in the lives of the ordained. Moreover, ordination was permanent. Once ordained, a priest was a priest forever.

Baptism and marriage are two other clear examples. Both were simple rituals that had permanent effects. Once baptized, you were a member of the Church and were subject to all of its rules, but you also thereby gained the privilege of receiving other sacraments for your sanctification and eternal salvation. Once married, you were joined to your spouse by a sacramental bond that was unbreakable until one of you died, but you also received the sacramental graces needed to be a faithful wife or husband. (Notice that being given the grace did not mean that you always used it. As with any gift, receiving it and using it are two different things.)

Everyone knew that confessing one's sins to a priest was needed to have serious sins forgiven, but even so, one had to perform works of penance to demonstrate one's repentance. Those penances also reduced the amount of punishment in the hereafter that one would incur for having sinned in this life. Indulgences could be gained by performing good works or by donating to charitable causes, and these could reduce the amount of time spent in purgatory before being allowed into heaven.

The holy sacrifice of the mass was offered by priests every day, making the salvation wrought by Christ's death on the cross available to all. Although few people could hear the words of the mass being spoken at the altar, everyone could hear the bell when it was rung, and everyone could see the Blessed Sacrament when it was lifted on high for all to adore. Prayers said at that moment were thought to be especially effective because God was close enough to hear them.

The point here is that the sacramental rituals did what they were supposed to do, and the effects were what everyone perceived them to be. Admittedly, the perception in question was magical perception, but it was no different from when a man was knighted by a king or when a nun professed her vows and entered a monastery. The ritual caused to happen what everyone expected it to do, and what everyone, in that sense, saw happening.

Only confirmation was a dishonest sacrament, and this because of its convoluted history. Originally a bishop's blessing administered after baptism, the blessing had become separated from the water ritual in the fourth century. When Christianity began to be favored by the Roman Emperors, there were more baptisms than a single bishop in each city could handle, so priests were allowed to do the baptizing but only the bishop was allowed to confirm the baptisms. Many people did not see the necessity of this confirmation, so for the most part it fell into disuse. In ninth century France, reform-minded bishops made an attempt to revive the practice, suggesting that it bestowed gifts of the Holy Spirit. Nevertheless, by the twelfth century, the sacrament was received primarily by those who wanted to enter clerical orders. An intellectual difficulty faced by the schoolmen was that they had to explain a second infusion of the Holy Spirit that had already been received in baptism. But the sacrament stayed in the ritual books, and it was performed even though it had no noticeable effects.

*

Not every performance of the medieval sacraments was honest.

People who know church history are aware that in the late Middle Ages, the institutional church was riddled with corruption and Christian rituals were often infused with superstition. A legalistic mentality began to set in during the fourteenth century, leading priests to believe that shortened rituals could still be effective as long as essential parts were not left out. In this way, they could collect many stipends for offering multiple masses for poor souls in purgatory while saving a great deal of time. In the same period, superstition ran rampant among the uneducated and largely illiterate laity. No only did they pay priests to offer frequent masses for their dearly departed, but they also began to buy prayer notes called indulgences, issued by unscrupulous bishops who wanted to raise money. Again the focus was on the souls in purgatory who needed to be freed from the agony of paying for their sins by suffering in the afterlife. Since no one could say how long a soul might have to make reparations in purgatory, no one could ever be sure that they had paid for enough masses or indulgences to free relatives and friends from torment. It was a fantastic marketing scheme.

Reform-minded intellectuals like John Wycliffe in England and Jan Hus in Bohemia protested against the corruption of Christianity by the clergy, but they were condemned as heretics. Wycliffe died before he could be executed, but Hus was burned at the stake. Only in the early sixteenth century did Martin Luther succeed in organizing a reform movement, in part because the German nobility were tired of seeing Rome siphon off money that could be better spent at home. Luther had originally wanted a reform of the church "in its head and members," but when the pope condemned him, he settled for a reform of the church without any particular head.

It took the Catholic Church 25 years to realize that the Protestants in northern Europe were never coming back. The bishops who met during the Council of Trent branded Protestant ideas as heretical, but they also acknowledged the mess that legalism and superstition had created in European Christianity. In response, they eliminated the sale of indulgences and set strict rules for the performance of the mass and the sacraments. They also demanded that priests be better trained, that the rule of celibacy be strictly enforced, and that bishops be more responsible in the administration of their dioceses. In time, the Catholic sacraments returned to honestly reflecting the teachings of the Church, and the Church lived up to the beliefs and values symbolized in its sacraments—at least as much as can be expected in a human institution.

For the most part, then, from the Council of Trent in the sixteenth century to the Second Vatican Council in the twentieth century, the sacraments were honest symbols of what was going on in the spiritual lives of Catholics and in the social life of the Church.

6

Honest Sacraments

THE SEPARATION BETWEEN CHURCH life and church rituals started happening after the Second Vatican Council.

For about four centuries, Roman Catholicism retained the medieval cultural form that had been established by the Council of Trent. The mass and sacraments were performed in Latin, Trinitarian doctrine was unquestioned, public devotions to the Blessed Virgin and the saints were pervasive, bishops and priests were revered as having supernatural powers, women and men in religious orders retained antiquated styles of dress, married Catholics never divorced, and, by and large, the Church's sacramental rituals operated as scholastic theology said they were supposed to.

In 1959, Pope John XXIII asked the world's Catholic bishops to convene in Rome to discuss the need for *aggiornamento*, that is, an updating of the Church's teachings and practices. He believed that the central truths of the faith were one thing and their cultural expression was another, so it would be possible to reformulate eternal verities in ways that could appeal to the modern mind. Laypeople for the most part supported this idea, and the Church's bishops succeeded in approving a raft of documents that gave Catholicism a less medieval and more modern look.

By the time the Second Vatican Council completed its work in 1965, it was hailed by most Catholics as a great success. Within a few years, the liturgy and sacraments were performed in languages that people around the world could understand, and the rites themselves were redesigned to take into account historical precedents and theological developments.

People were encouraged to participate more fully in the Church's religious ceremonies, both by singing and by reciting prayer responses. When new churches were built, they had simpler and cleaner architectural lines, and older churches were remodeled so the priest at the altar would face the people instead of having his back to them. Church music also became more contemporary, as did the dress styles of those in religious orders.

For about a decade, it seemed that the Council had succeeded. Catholics still believed what they used to, but now they could be modern as well. Their worship took on a contemporary air, and they engaged in serious ecumenical dialogue, attempting to understand Protestants and Jews instead of trying to convert them to Catholicism. This in turn led to a new interest in studying the Bible and applying the scriptures to daily living, as Evangelicals often do. A revival of interest in charismatic spirituality led to the formation of ecumenical prayer groups and to holding charismatic prayer meetings with hundreds and sometimes thousands of people speaking in tongues and praising the Lord.

*

But it was not to last.

The sixties and seventies were times of great social change in Europe, America and elsewhere in the world where Catholics lived. The institutional Church, which had been solid and unchanging for centuries, began to experience cracks in its traditional structures. In an era of social liberation, priests asked to be able to marry, and when they were denied, they left the priesthood. Many nuns also left the convent, and those who remained in religious orders left the traditional fields of teaching and nursing to engage in a variety of social ministries from helping the poor to lobbying in Washington. Married people too preferred seeking personal fulfillment to fulfilling marital obligations, and within a short time the divorce rate of Catholics equaled that of other Americans. The women's liberation movement not only raised women's consciousness, it also encouraged women to seek their own careers and earn a living outside of marriage.

Developments in psychology provided deeper insights into human motivation, leading moral theologians to question whether missing mass or disobeying other church rules could truly constitute mortal sins. With fewer sins to confess before receiving communion, Saturday confession lines dwindled and then disappeared entirely. By the same token, participation in holy communion, which previously had been rare even among the devout, became commonplace. But the renewed liturgy, which called for hymn singing even during the reception of communion, made it more difficult for Catholics to experience the presence of Christ in the Eucharist on a regular basis.

The election of Pope John Paul II in 1978 ushered in three decades of conservative reaction to the liberal adaptations of the sixties and seventies. The new pope restricted the independence of bishops that had expanded after the Council, insisting that they adhere to Roman norms even in Africa and Asia. The rate of men leaving the priesthood eventually leveled off, but the number of young men entering the seminary did not increase, adding to the burden on older clergy and leading to the closing of once vibrant parishes.

Whereas canon lawyers had been expanding the grounds for annulment so divorced people could remarry and remain within the Church, pastoral concerns among the hierarchy gave way to legalistic ones, and people who found it hard to obtain annulments simply married outside the Church. In parishes that remained open, many had empty pews even on Sundays, and gray heads often outnumbered those of young adults and families.

*

Unintentionally, then, the Church's sacraments became dishonest.

Stories like those mentioned in the introduction to this book became commonplace, so they need not be repeated here. Nor need those stories be bolstered with statistics, which are readily available to anyone who wants to do the research. The simple fact is that, although the Catholic Church changed around the edges, the core of its sacramental theology remained rooted in medieval experience and Aristotelian thinking.

The result is a church whose ritual practices are deeply disconnected from the social and spiritual experiences of many of its members. Not all, certainly, for there are still conservative Catholics whose faith life is nourished by the traditional sacraments, either as revised after Vatican II or as practiced in Latin before the Council. And not all, because vibrant parishes can be found in North America, Europe, Latin America and elsewhere when the life of the parish breathes vitality into standard liturgical forms. But in many places, if not most, the official sacraments have ceased informing the spiritual lives of Catholics. Most of those who still call themselves Catholics develop their religious consciousness outside of church, and they bring that consciousness to ceremonies that they cannot internally connect with.

If honest rituals are those in which the reality being celebrated is present where the ritual is being performed, we have to admit that this is not the case in most Catholic parishes. What are celebrated are not experienced realities but religious beliefs—beliefs in metaphysical realities that are, by definition, beyond human experience. The salvation that baptism is said to bestow is not something that can be felt, especially by infants whose range of experience is severely limited. The gift of the Spirit that confirmation is said to confer is not something to be experienced but only to be believed. The divine forgiveness that reconciliation is said to offer has to be believed in, but once accepted, it can bring feelings of relief and gratefulness. The divine healing that anointing is said to offer likewise needs to be believed in, although afterwards it can engender feelings of inner strengthening and peace. The marital grace that marriage is said to bestow has to be believed in because it seems to have no noticeable effect on a couple's relationship. The supernatural powers that ordination is said to confer have to be believed in, but when they are simultaneously believed in by priest and people, Catholics can perceive the metaphysical effects of priestly actions. The presence of Christ in holy communion is something that has to be believed in because his actual presence is difficult to detect amid the motion and noise of Sunday mass.

Honest sacraments are not those that celebrate beliefs but those that celebrate lived realities—spiritual realities in the sense described in chapter one.

Christmas and Easter are great examples of beliefs that are celebrated in the absence of spiritual realities. Christmas celebrates the birth of Christ, bringing peace on earth and goodwill to all, but peace in families and cities and nations is too often an elusive ideal rather than an experienced reality. Easter celebrates the resurrection of Christ, bringing victory over death, but the victory is hollow when the death is that of a loved one, when we feel threatened by an epidemic, or when the noise of war gets close. We try hard to celebrate ideas, and we sometimes convince ourselves that ideas are real, but in our heart of hearts we realize that ideas fall short of reality.

*

What would honest sacraments look like?

There is no way to answer this question. Sacraments are symbols—ritual symbols, to be sure, but symbols nonetheless. What makes a symbol honest is not what it looks like but whether or not it refers to something real.

Remember that we talked about words being symbols that refer to something other than themselves. By extension, combinations of words that are sentences are honest (which is also to say, truthful) when they refer to states of affairs that correspond to statements. If I say, "I am typing this sentence," when I am actually doing so, then my statement is true and the sentence is honest. Were I to say, "I am standing on the moon," when I am not doing that, then my statement is false and the sentence is not honest. It is not honest because its referent is non-existent.

Now, sentences can be written (or spoken) in any language whatever, and what makes them honest symbols is not what they look like—the appearance of the words—but the presence or absence of a referent. If a referent is present, I can speak honestly about it. If a referent is not present, I can speak about it, but not honestly.

To understand sacramental honesty, therefore, we need to begin with what sacraments refer to, and discuss those spiritual realities. Only after that would it be appropriate to discuss the symbolic expression of spiritual realities in religious rituals.

*

Where to begin?

When discussing the Catholic sacraments, it is common to begin with baptism, since that is a sacrament of initiation. Ceremonies of initiation, however, present a problem in that they necessarily refer to the reality or realities into which one is ritually initiated.

We can say that baptism ritualizes initiation into the church, but what does that mean today? In the past, when baptism was thought to bestow supernatural gifts (also known as sacramental graces or theological virtues) that made Christians metaphysically different from everyone else, it was possible to define church as the assembly of the baptized. The baptized were those who were metaphysically marked as belonging to Christ, who were given the theological virtues of faith, hope and love, who were thereby able to go to heaven and experience the beatific vision, and who had both the right and the ability to receive other sacraments. But if scholastic theology has been discredited, we cannot say this any more.

Is being a member of the church the same as being a member of a club, especially a club whose members have no rights or responsibilities? It would seem that way, because people who are members of the Catholic Church through baptism do not seem to have to do anything. They do not even have to go to church, that is, to attend church services. The hierarchy would like to say that only Catholics, and indeed Catholics in good standing, can receive holy communion, but this rule is unenforceable. Anyone can attend a Catholic mass and go up for communion if they want to. All that prevents people from doing so is self-imposed obedience to a church rule.

When it comes down to it, therefore, baptized Catholics have no responsibilities and therefore no rights. They don't have to do anything to be called Catholic, and they have no rights that are different from the rights of people who are not Catholic. True, some rights are granted by canon law, such as the right to receive other sacraments, but even these rights can be denied by the institution. You cannot get married or be ordained in the Church without the institution's permission.

There is an old saying that sitting in church does not make you a Christian any more than sitting in a garage makes you a car. In the present context, I think we can add that being baptized does not make you a Christian any more than being rained on makes you a flower.

✶

Honest rites of passage have to be initiations into something real.

When someone is inducted into the military, their life changes. This is also true of two sacramental rites, namely, ordination and marriage. Those church ceremonies change the social status of those who go through them, and they give people rights and responsibilities that they did not have prior to the ceremony.

Upon reflection, however, this is less true today of the wedding ceremony than it was in ages past. Many couples today live together before marriage, and they may even have children together. So the wedding as a rite of passage into married life is not the life-changing transition ritual that it used to be.

This leaves us with ordination as a paradigm and a model, of sorts, for understanding religious rites of passage today. Even so, we cannot take ordination as it is currently practiced as paradigmatic because it is based on priesthood in the Middle Ages, which entailed magical thinking as interpreted by Aristotelian science. Instead of repeating what was said by the schoolmen, we need to do for our own times what the schoolmen did for their times, which was to understand the nature and purpose of church ceremonies.

Whereas the schoolmen used Aristotelian science, we should use contemporary science, especially the social sciences of psychology, sociology and ritual studies. Not that we have to bring everything in those sciences to bear on our understanding of sacraments, but there are some basics that are quite helpful. For example, both sociology and ritual studies tell us that rites of passage always involve a *from* and a *to*, a *status ante* and a *status post*. Since most of the Catholic sacraments are rites of passage, they need to celebrate genuine changes in people's lives.

*

Envisioning honest sacraments will not entail doing sacramental or liturgical theology.

Sacramental theology and liturgical theology are academic disciplines that reflect on church rituals, understand them in light of scripture and tradition, and explain them in such a way that non-theologians can understand what any particular sacrament is about. What those sacraments will look like in the future, however, and how they will function in a variety of cultural and social settings is something that remains to be seen.

The premise of our argument is that, in order for sacraments to be honest rituals, they need to celebrate spiritual realities that are actually present in the community. And if the ceremony in question is a rite of passage, it needs to facilitate or at least to celebrate a genuine change in people's lives.

Once there is a sacramental rite or ceremonial script, and once it is implemented in a sacramental ritual or ceremonial performance, then it can be reflected on and explained. Not before. Part of the problem with the sacraments today is that theological explanations are given before rituals are performed. Before confirmation, children are told that they are going to receive the gift of the Holy Spirit, even if they get nothing out of the ceremony. Before the wedding, couples are told that they are going to be married forever, even if they eventually divorce. These are just some of the clearest examples. To be honest, theological explanations need to reflect on what actually happens during a church ritual and on what can be expected to actually happen afterwards.

An example may make this clearer. In one of my favorite books, *Christianity Rediscovered* by Vincent Donovan, the author describes a ritual of forgiveness practiced by the Masai tribe in Africa when he was a missionary there. If a man offends another man in some way, and then wants to be forgiven, he goes to the one he offended and asks for the spittle of forgiveness. If the offended man is inclined to grant the petition, he spits on the one asking for forgiveness. Symbolically, he is "sharing his water" with the other man, for in the dry country where the Masai live, water is a precious commodity.

I don't know if women practice this ritual. It seems to be such a guy thing. But it is a clear example of a ritual that is both honest and culturally quite strange. It shows an honest asking for forgiveness and an honest ritual of forgiveness, for the one being asked is under no obligation to grant the request. Only if he feels it in his heart to forgive does he ritually demonstrate the spiritual reality that cannot be seen by the petitioner.

If the spiritual realities that are celebrated in the traditional sacraments are allowed to be ritualized in other cultures, they may sometimes turn out to be as strange as the spittle of forgiveness. The sacramental forms invented or adapted by people in other cultures are not things that should be determined by Westerners. Ritual is a symbolic means of expression and communication, just as language is a symbolic means of expression and communication. We do not tell people in other cultures what language to speak, so we should not tell people in other cultures what ritual to use.

Just as the same ideas can be communicated in diverse languages, so also the same spiritual realities can be celebrated in diverse rituals. Moreover, the theological explanation of those rituals is something that should be done after the rituals are developed. It is not something that should be done beforehand.

*

What are the spiritual realities that should be celebrated in church rituals?

In chapter one, we talked about a number of such realities. Acceptance, belonging, community, empowerment, repentance, compassion, forgiveness, healing, strengthening, commitment, fidelity, love, caring, self-giving, serving, ministering—these are all values and principles that, when practiced, are realities that are found in people's lives. Looking at the list, they seem to be ones that are most closely related to the traditional sacraments.

Can you think of any that I have left out? Which sacraments would they be associated with?

Of course, this is not the full extent of experienced and experienceable spiritual realities. I can also think of courage, generosity, creativity, cooperation, optimism, fairness, justice, truthfulness, patience, reliability, and trust. These are all values for living and principles of behavior that make living together possible and that in the long run make life enjoyable. Some people would also call them virtues because they are strengths of character. They can also be thought of as life skills. Human beings are not born with these skills, and not everyone acquires them. Individuals have to develop them over time, either deliberately or in order to cope with situations that call for them.

This is not an exhaustive list. What other life values or virtues can you think of?

Social organizations besides churches may facilitate and celebrate virtues as well. Police, fire and military organizations value and reward courage, reliability, loyalty, and even risk-taking. Sports teams value and reward reliability, cooperation, passion, and excellence in performance. Businesses value and reward creativity, entrepreneurship, tenaciousness and optimism. The entertainment industry values originality, genuineness, and artistic excellence. There is hardly a virtue that is not recognized and celebrated in some area of human endeavor.

Think of an activity in which you have been coached or have coached others. What were some of the ritual ways or showing encouragement or appreciation for the development of skills? It could be a ritual as simple as a pat on the back or saying, "You go, girl!" Try to name some of the spiritual realities that you had in mind when you have done this for someone who was learning a skill.

Remember that church rituals that are rites of passage must refer to and celebrate spiritual realities that are present in those who are being celebrated if the rituals are to be honest.

*

Not all spiritual realities are positive values and principles. There are some that are negative.

Besides virtues there are vices. Besides acquired habits that enhance life, there are those that diminish life or destroy it. Again, no one is born with these abilities, so they have to be acquired, and they have to be developed.

Some of the negative qualities that people can develop are cowardice, deceitfulness, selfishness, disloyalty, impatience, callousness, recklessness, and arrogance. The so-called seven deadly sins are actually vices. Traditionally these are listed as pride, greed, lust, wrath, gluttony, envy and sloth.

Spiritual realities such as these are never celebrated in rituals, although they are sometimes glorified in works of fiction. Nor is there any religion that promotes them. Any religion that tried to promote them would soon self-destruct because its adherents would be literally vicious, that is, full of the vices just mentioned.

Those who accuse a religion—whether it be Christianity, Judaism, Islam, Hinduism, or any other—of promoting evil do not understand religion. They may sound knowledgeable, but they actually do not know what they are talking about.

Even gangs and cartels do not promote vices among their members. If they did so, they would be promoting their own undoing. The certainly utilize and reward vicious individuals, but what they honor and celebrate are basic virtues such as loyalty and obedience in their members, as well as helpful virtues such as cleverness and bravery.

If you have read any of the Godfather novels or watched any of the movies, can you see how this is true? How does gangster fiction glorify the honor code of criminals?

One definition of addiction is a habit that causes momentary satisfaction but that ultimately leads to death. Since vices are forms of habitual behavior, they can also be regarded as addictions. Much is known today about the physiology of addiction, but the biological basis of the addictive process does not negate its being a spiritual reality as well. Every idea and every ideal, every value and every principle that we have is a spiritual reality that has a biological basis. You cannot think without using brain cells.

*

Back to sacraments.

Nothing would prevent a religion from celebrating any of the virtues just discussed. The Romans, for example, celebrated courage and military prowess when they honored Mars, the god of war. Buddhists celebrate and promote compassion, but I do not know of any ceremonies that refer to it directly. Followers of Confucius value benevolence, integrity, loyalty, uprightness, and the promotion of social harmony, but these virtues are taught rather than celebrated in rituals, although they are implied in the veneration of ancestors.

Taking the Catholic tradition as our guide, let us imagine some ways to ritualize Christian values and gospel principles, especially as rites of passage analogous to the traditional sacraments. To begin, we can look at the value of self-giving in caring for and caring about others.

The gospels make it clear that Jesus was not focused on himself. Although centuries of Christianity have focused on Jesus as the Christ, as savior, as Lord, and as Son of God, Jesus himself focused his attention on others. In the synoptic gospels, he appears as one driven to tell people the good news that God is in charge, and that if they let God rule the way they live, they will be saved from the many ways that they mess up their lives.

The Greek word, *agápē*, is usually translated as "love" in the New Testament, but it really means care or caring. When Jesus tells his followers to love one another (John 13:34–35), he is telling them to care about each other and to take care of one another. Even when he tells them to love their enemies (Matthew 5:44), he is not telling them to like the people who don't like them. Rather, he is telling his followers to care about people who don't care about them, and to take care of them if they are in need, for doing that is the best way to get them to change hateful and suspicious attitudes.

Putting the notion of caring alongside the notion of living under God's reign or rule, we can say that the fundamental teaching of Jesus was that God wants people to take care of one another, so if they actually live that way, they will be living according to God's rules. The "great commandment" to love God above all and to love one's neighbor as oneself (Matthew 22:37–40) actually means to care about what God wants, and to take care of those around you the same way you take care of yourself.

At one point, Jesus says that treating others the way you want to be treated sums up the Law and the Prophets (Matthew 7:12). Again, the emphasis is on doing, not on liking. *Agápē* is not a feeling word; it is an action word. Caring about and taking care of are not things that you feel; they are things that you do. In story after story, Jesus cares about the poor, the sick, the lame, the deaf and dumb, the spiritually tormented, and even about people who are grieving.

ORDINATION

How can this value be ritualized?

One obvious way that caring gets ritualized is in ordination to ministry. People can feel called to serve others full time and professionally within and on behalf of a community. For many churches, this entails years of training in theology, spirituality, counseling, preaching, and community leadership.

The ritual for celebrating entrance into the ministry of leadership is traditionally known as ordination, from the Latin word *ordo* meaning rank or order. In ancient and medieval times, there were different levels of church service, and entrance into each level (deacon, priest, bishop, and others) was accomplished through a separate rite of passage. Originally, any such ritual was called an ordination, including elevation to the order of abbot or abbess in monasteries, but in the twelfth century the term got restricted to priestly ordination.

During the first centuries of Christianity, older women were ordained to the order of widows, who attended to the physical needs of women and children. Deaconesses, or women ordained to the order of deacon, also led women in prayer and had certain liturgical functions. Cultural sexism of the ancient and medieval worlds limited women to serving women and children, but women nonetheless had leadership and liturgical roles that were later denied them.

Under the influence of Aristotelian science, according to which special powers were needed to do anything that was beyond natural abilities, the priesthood was defined in terms of the priestly powers to forgive sins, to turn bread and wine into the body and blood of Christ, and to pass these powers to other men through ordination.

Today, using contemporary social sciences to understand what happens in ordination, there is no need to invoke metaphysical concepts and supernatural powers. The power that a priest receives to preside over community worship is analogous to the power that a judge receives to preside over court proceedings, or the power that a conductor receives to preside over an orchestra. Such power can be understood as arising from social consent, just as a government derives its power from the consent of the governed. If people withdraw their consent, the people holding government offices lose their power. Any school teacher understands that if the children in her class refuse to be obedient, she has lost her power over them.

Removing the concept of supernatural power makes it easier to understand priesthood in terms of the skills needed to do well as someone who presides at worship, who preaches during the eucharistic liturgy and other services, who administers a parish, who has a pastoral relationship with members of the community, and who is the representative of the institutional church at the local level. Moreover, understanding ministry in terms of skills undercuts any sexism that would exclude candidates on the basis of gender, and it undercuts any bias against homosexual candidates. Applying for the priesthood is analogous to applying for any other professional position: if you have the skills, you are eligible for the job.

Removing the concept of supernatural power also removes any justification for making priesthood a lifetime commitment. In the Aristotelian scheme of things, receiving such powers was a permanent change in the soul of the ordained, so that even priests who left the ministry were regarded as retaining their priestly powers. It was analogous to a boxer losing his license to fight even though he still had the ability to fight. In today's society, however, people are allowed to change professions if they want to. This is already the case with Protestant ministers, and there is no reason why it should not be the case with Catholic priests.

If ordination did not entail a lifetime commitment, it would be easier to recruit men and women into the priesthood. Protestant churches and denominations often have more ministers than they need, which is the opposite of the situation in the Catholic Church. Removing the requirement of celibacy could have a similar effect. A celibate clergy is an anachronism from the past. No profession today requires it. Of course, men and women could still choose a life of celibacy, living in community with other men and women in a monastery or cloister, or if they simply prefer to remain unmarried, as some dedicated professionals do.

MARRIAGE

Marriage is another sacrament that celebrates the same values as ordination.

In the Middle Ages and even in the Tridentine church, marriage was a family arrangement. This is far different from today, when marriage is a couple's decision.

One reason why men and women in ages past could not divorce is that most marriages were arranged by their parents. Since people did not decide to get married, they could not decide to get unmarried. The social structure did not allow it, and the Church's prohibition of divorce basically ratified what was a social reality.

Yet it was not this way from the beginning. The apostle Paul allowed for the possibility of divorce in certain circumstances (1 Corinthians 7:15), and divorce was allowed by law in the Roman Empire even after Christianity became the state religion. Ending a marriage for an unjust reason was regarded as a sin, but it was a sin that could be forgiven, and remarriage was possible. Some bishops in the patristic period cited Mark 10:11–12 to prove that divorce is a sin, while others cited Matthew 5:32 to prove that sometimes it wasn't. Still, it is a matter of historical fact that Christians in the Latin church could divorce and remarry for eleven centuries, and that Christians in the Greek Orthodox tradition have always been able to do so.

In the twelfth century, two factors led to marriage being declared indissoluble. The first was a fundamentalistic reading of Mark 10:11–12 and Luke 16:18, both of which condemn divorce. The exceptions in Matthew 5:32 and 1 Corinthians 7:15 were obviously ignored. The second was Aristotelian metaphysics, which interpreted the bond of marriage as more than a legal contract or emotional relationship. The bond was conceived as analogous to the invisible sign received in baptism, the seal of the Spirit received in confirmation, and the priestly character received in ordination. Any change in the soul was regarded as permanent because the soul was not subject to decay. The fact that this indissoluble bond was said to dissolve when one of the spouses died was conveniently overlooked.

The schoolmen, it could be said, accepted the impossibility of divorce in the Middle Ages and came up with scriptural and theological justifications for the medieval practice.

Moreover, it could be argued that marriage in ancient and medieval times was a different institution from what it is today, even though the word "marriage" is applied to both. We get a glimpse of what counted as marriage in the ancient world from the Epistle to the Ephesians, where women are told to submit their husband in all things, and men are told to take care of their wife the way they care for their own body (Ephesians 5:22–33).

Clearly, this was an unequal relationship in which the women did all the submitting and the men did all the caring. The arranged marriages in medieval times were little different. A woman lost her identity by losing her personal property and even her family name when she was turned over to the man selected by her parents. As late as the early twentieth century, the children of a marriage belonged to the father, not to the couple.

Until fairly recently then, marriage was a social institution in which parents insured the continuation of the family name and the perseveration of the family property by selecting healthy wives for their sons. Daughters did not provide the same advantage, but hopefully they could be married off to respectable and responsible husbands, and they would produce children that would increase the wealth of the extended family in the long run. In this social context, it was understandable that the Catholic Church taught that the purpose of marriage was the procreation of children.

It ain't so, today. Arranged marriages are out. For better or worse, women and men select their own spouses. Statistically, about half of them make a mistake the first time around, and the statistics for second marriages are not any better. Moreover, they do not marry in order to have children. Some marry with no intention to have children, and some have children without marrying. Children are not a necessary part of marriage any more.

Today, many people marry for love—not in the sense of *agápē* or caring for the other, but in the sense of romantic love, otherwise known as infatuation. When the feeling wears off (as it eventually must), the love dies, and unless it is replaced by something more stable, the marriage dies and the couple divorces.

Marriage counselors say that a key factor in marital satisfaction is good communication skills. Couples who can communicate their feelings and thoughts clearly while trying to be open and honest with each other increase their chances of maintaining a happy and lasting relationship. Another important factor is giving more importance to your partner's needs than to your own wants. If you want lasting companionship, it is necessary to be a good companion.

Increasingly, today's ideal of companionate marriage begins to look like the biblical virtue of *agápē*. Jesus said that the greatest love is laying down one's life for a friend (John 15:13). When two people are willing and able to give top priority to the well-being of their partner, they are doing in practice what is called for by the scriptural metaphor of laying down one's life for someone else.

Such a relationship can also be thought of in terms of ministry and service. A couple in a truly companionate marriage minister to each other, and they try to be of service to each other. It is a mutual relationship of self-giving. It is a two-way ministry.

Looking at the wedding ceremony as a celebration of *agápē*, not in the abstract but in the concrete sense that here are two people who want the best for each other, who are willing to put selfishness aside for the good of their partner, it is certainly an honest ritual. It celebrates a spiritual reality that is present in the hearts and minds of two individuals who at this moment are willing to pledge their fidelity and support to each other. Analogous to the relationship of a minister to a community, marriage creates a relationship in which both parties minister and are ministered to.

Regarded in terms of the spiritual reality that is at the heart of a mutually supportive relationship, Christian marriage has little to do with the physical realities of gender and sexual activity. In the past, when the purpose of marriage was the continuation of a family through the procreation of children, marriage could only be between a man and a woman. Today, when the purpose of a wedding is to celebrate a relationship of mutual caring, there is no need for the partners to have different genders, and there is no need for them to be able to engage in genital sex. It is possible, therefore, for a church to celebrate the marriages of homosexual couples and of disabled persons who cannot have sexual intercourse.

RECONCILIATION

Penance was once a culturally appropriate sacrament.

The Christian consciousness of sin in the Middle Ages was shaped by medieval culture. Medieval Europe was a stable and stratified society— stable because society changed imperceptibly from one decade to the next, and stratified because there was no social mobility. Between Charlemagne's Holy Roman Empire in the ninth century and the early Renaissance in the fifteenth century, rulers came and went, wars were won and lost, boundaries were drawn and redrawn, but for most people most of the time, these far-away events meant little change in their lives. Cities thought nothing of taking a century to build a cathedral, with stone masons and other artisans passing the work from father to son and to grandson. Nobles were nobles, and peasants were peasants. There was no middle class.

If individuals changed their station in life, it was almost always facilitated by a rite of passage. Boys and girls married and became husbands and wives. Those who did not marry took vows and entered a monastery or convent. The clergy advanced from one holy order to another through a series of ordination rituals. Social rules were clear, and behavior that violated someone's honor had to punished or atoned for.

In such a culture, sin is the breaking of a rule, and rule-breaking can be forgiven only the admission of guilt and the performance of a penalty. There are rules for the confession of wrongdoing and the performance of penances. In the early Middle Ages, confession could be made to a layperson, usually a monk or a nun. In the twelfth century, however, the rules changed and only priests could listen to the confession of sins. For a while, penitential books provided lists of sins and corresponding penances for confessors without much imagination or pastoral sense. But the important thing to understand was that rule-breaking was a violation of social norms, and the culture provided rituals for returning society to stability. The Catholic Church, being part of this culture, conceived of sin as rule breaking and offered the sacrament of penance as a ritual means for seeking forgiveness and receiving pardon from God.

In such a society, there is no such thing as a private sin. Any behavior that violates sexual norms also violates the moral fabric of society, so it has to be stopped and it has to be atoned for. The Bible was invoked to support such norms. For example, Genesis 38:8–9 was invoked to prove that masturbation is a sin.

This medieval conception of sin and its remission through the confession of guilt and the performance of penitential works lasted into modern times because the Church retained its medieval cultural form while the world around it changed. By the mid-twentieth century, however, some moral theologians were using the social sciences to understand motivation and behavior, and they were suggesting that breaking a church rule such as eating meat on Friday or missing mass on Sunday might not be a serious sin.

The Catholic consciousness of sin did not begin to change until after the Second Vatican Council, when the name of the sacrament was changed from penance to reconciliation, and when the rite allowed for a meeting of priest and penitent that was more like counseling than confession. A development that accelerated the change was the pope's pronouncement in 1968 that artificial birth control is a sin—eight years after the invention of the contraceptive pill. Catholic women who were using the pill, sometimes after being assured by a priest that they could follow their conscience, rejected the teaching of the magisterium and stopped going to confession. So did many Catholics who agreed that committing a sin had to be more than simply breaking a rule.

*

Reconciliation means more than asking God for forgiveness.

Certainly there are Catholics today for whom the current sacrament of reconciliation is helpful. They may feel that they have violated God's law and that they need to seek divine forgiveness. They may feel burdened by guilt for having hurt someone, and they seek the sacrament to clear their conscience. Or they may seek counseling from a priest in the privacy of a confessional for any of a number of reasons. If they ask for forgiveness, the priest grants them absolution and asks them to say some prayers as works of penance.

Not a whole lot to celebrate there. Which is one reason why the sacrament has fallen into disuse. Keeping it on the books as a major Catholic ritual is therefore somewhat dishonest. According to the Catechism of the Catholic Church, reconciliation is an important ritual practice, but clearly it is not.

Might there be some way to re-imagine the sacrament to make it an honest ritual?

Remember that our criterion for an honest ritual is one in which the spiritual reality being celebrated is actually present among those who are participating in it. Here it means that if reconciliation is to be honestly celebrated, it has to be really happening. At the very least, it has to have happened recently.

A theological theme that emerged during Vatican II is that, besides the seven liturgical sacraments, the Church is itself a sacrament of Christ. In other words, when people look at what the Church is doing—whether it be the ecclesiastical institution or the people of God, as the council liked to call the Church's members—they ought to be able to perceive what Christ is doing in the world. In other words, if the institution and its members are truly symbols of Jesus Christ in the world, others ought to be able to sense that they are doing God's work.

Needless to say, this is often not the case. The Church and its members are commonly perceived as acting in their own self-interest, and even creating antagonism in the world rather than reconciliation.

So what might the Church do differently? It would have to devote time and energy to bring about reconciliation between individuals, between groups, and maybe even between countries.

At the parish level, it would have to devote resources, both money and personnel, to reconciliation within families: between husbands and wives, between parents and teenagers, between siblings who are angry with each other, and perhaps even between extended family members. Such a ministry of reconciliation would have to be a recognized department in the parish, with its own ministers and resources, and with a substantial budget.

This may seem like a totally off-the-wall suggestion, but I have seen it at work. Earlier in my life, I knew about a Protestant church that did exactly this. The church had a full-time pastoral counselor whose job was not to counsel church members directly, but to train volunteers to do elementary counseling, usually through active listening. The volunteers were also trained to recognize when they encountered problems that were out of their depth, and to refer them to the church's professional counselor, who in turn referred them to professionals in the area who could address their needs over an extended course of counseling and therapy. If people could not afford professional counseling, the church had a fund to pay for it.

Hiring an extra full-time minister costs money. Training dozens of lay ministers and ministering to their needs took time, energy, and more money. But the church was prosperous because those whose emotional and spiritual needs were met by the ministry of counseling expressed their gratefulness through generous financial support of the church and by inviting other people to avail themselves of the church's service. Many of those who were helped became members of that congregation.

Since that church was not a liturgical church, it had no ritual for celebrating reconciliation events. But since it was an evangelical church, it had a tradition of people offering personal testimony during the Sunday service. Testimonies of reconciliation drew applause and congratulations—which are rituals of sorts, when you think about it.

*

What about reaching out beyond the parish membership?

We read stories about people reaching out to gang members, trying to negotiate a reduction or cessation of violence between rival groups. Sometimes it entails finding jobs for young people or helping them complete their education because teenagers and young adults often join gangs because they have nothing better to do.

There are other instances of groups opposing each other and perhaps even arguing about it. Environmentalists and developers, workers and employers, people and police, new immigrants and long-time residents are groups that come immediately to mind.

The work of mediation and reconciliation is not unknown to social workers, counselors and negotiators, so I am not talking here about work that has never been done. I am only talking about work that the institutional church has never seen as part of its mission, perhaps because the word "reconciliation" has been relegated to the confession box. Much good could be done if a diocese started thinking out of the box.

One possibility could be the promotion of what is called restorative practices or restorative justice. The main way that our society deals with children and adults who harm others by bullying, stealing and causing physical harm is through the criminal justice system. Bad behavior is called a crime and punished by various incarcerations ranging from detentions in schools to imprisonment in jails and penitentiaries. Incarceration, however, does nothing to heal the hurt that was caused or to repair the breakdown in society. Restorative justice, on the other hand, is a process that brings offenders and victims together, that helps offenders to feel the pain they have caused, and to begin to make reparations to their victims. Restorative practices have already begun to be used in school systems, replacing detention and expulsion with a process of consciousness raising and conscience formation. Surely these are values with which the Church can identify.

Engaging in the work of reconciliation between individuals and groups in the community is a larger task than a parish can take on, but it is not beyond the resources of a diocese. Catholic dioceses are for the most part unknown to people who are not Catholics, and they are often invisible even to Catholics. People may know who the local bishop is, but they usually do not know much beyond that, except when a scandal breaks into the news or when a diocese has to pay a large financial settlement.

Wouldn't the local church become a more visible sacrament of reconciliation if it engaged in the work of reconciliation and then celebrated its successes in church services in which people told their stories in a way that might also inspire others?

ANOINTING

What does anointing have to do with healing?

In ancient times, olive oil could be applied to dry skin and bruises to hasten the healing process. In a famous parable of Jesus, a compassionate Samaritan pours wine and oil on a man who was beaten by robbers and left for dead. Before the invention of modern medicines, vegetable oil and alcohol from fermented fruit played a large role in healing.

In addition, faith came into the healing process more than it does today. Jesus sometimes told the people he healed that their faith had saved them, and scholars speculate that part of Jesus' ministry is what is today called faith healing. But Jesus was not the only one. In every pre-modern culture there are people who seem to have a reputation for healing, and they are sought out by people who are sick. Often such healers lay hands on those who are ill, invoking whatever powers they believe are able to make people well. If the sick cannot be brought to them, they might impart a blessing on water or oil that is then taken to the sick person in the expectation that healing power would be thereby bestowed. It is magical thinking, but it sometimes works. Among early Christians, healers were more likely to be monks or hermits than priests or bishops.

In medieval Europe, many of those reputed to have healing powers were women. Initially, these would have been wiccans or practitioners of local nature religions—women who were persecuted for being witches even after their tribes had been converted to Christianity. In the ninth century, the creation of a healing ritual to be performed by a group of priests was partly a response to this pagan practice. The Christian ritual never caught on, however, because people had to bring their sick to a monastery or church to be prayed over. Only the nobles with access to a private chapel could avail themselves of this service. Even so, given the absence of modern medicine, people often died after being prayed over and anointed, so by the thirteenth century the rite was no longer a sacrament of healing but a sacrament of preparation for entrance into the next life.

The Council of Trent in the sixteenth century modernized the sacrament that was then called extreme unction or last anointing, simplifying the rite, allowing it to be done by a single priest, and allowing the sacrament to be brought to homes, hospitals and wherever it was needed. This form of the sacrament is remembered by older Catholics as one of the last rites, the other two being a last confession and a final reception of communion.

The Second Vatican Council restored the original purpose of the sacrament and changed its name back to anointing of the sick. It took a while for Catholics to get accustomed to the change because they were so used to regarding it as a sacrament for the dying, but by now the purpose of the ritual is pretty clear to most Catholic laity. This change in attitude is due in part to the expansion of the liturgical rite. It can now be performed in church either as a stand-alone ritual or in conjunction with what is unofficially called a healing mass to which the sick and elderly in a parish are invited. Anointing ceremonies for groups are also common in Catholic nursing homes and retirement homes, which might offer healing services for the residents on a regular basis. People who are ill for a long period of time can receive the anointing at home, and some churches offer the anointing of the sick after mass to people who are going to undergo surgery.

The sacrament in its present form is an honest ritual because it prays for healing without promising it, and because it communicates the concern of the institutional church for the well-being of its members. In addition, people who are anointed sometimes report spiritual benefits such as support by their community, acceptance of their illness, or reduced anxiety in the face of surgery.

Nevertheless, the Church is not honest in restricting the ministry of this sacrament to priests. When the liturgical ritual was created in the ninth century, it was justified as the fulfillment of a biblical mandate that priests should anoint the sick. This was, however, a misinterpretation of James 5:14, which says that presbyters ought to anoint and pray over the sick. In the Middle Ages, the Latin word *presbyter* was understood to refer to a priest, but scholars today say that the original reference is to a community elder who was not a priest in the medieval or modern sense of the term. Since church leaders are well aware of contemporary scripture scholarship, restriction of this ministry to the clergy is intellectually dishonest.

The restriction is also pastorally insensitive. Many Catholics do not receive the anointing of the sick because there are many more sick people than there are priests, and the problem is constantly exacerbated by the declining number of ordained priests. All too often, priests who visit the sick in hospitals cannot make genuinely pastoral visits because they need to see a number of patients in a limited amount of time. They can become, in the worst sense of the term, sacrament dispensers who engage in magical thinking.

There is no valid theological reason for restricting this ministry to priests, and there are sound pastoral reasons for extending the use of the liturgical rite to deacons and lay people who are hospital chaplains or lay ministers in a parish. The restriction only serves to deprive the sick and elderly of a ministry that could offer them spiritual comfort.

In fact, the church in the wider sense of the people of God has taken the initiative to disregard ecclesiastical barriers to anointing the sick. In addition to praying for and praying with the sick in homes and hospitals, they use what is called healing touch or therapeutic touch in their ministry, holding the hand of a patient or laying a hand on the patient's head or shoulder while praying for them. Some hospital chaplains even carry a vial of oil for Catholic patients who ask to be anointed but do not realize that a priest is unavailable. This practice can be genuinely sacramental if it gives comfort and assurance to those who need it. Shortly after Vatican II, a few creative bishops even composed diocesan rites for deacons to anoint the sick, but this practice disappeared under the conservative popes in the late twentieth and early twenty-first century.

There is also the larger issue of the sacramentality of the Church, which has been emphasized since the Second Vatican Council. But honestly, is the Catholic Church a sign of God's caring and healing power in the world today?

During the Middle Ages, there were no hospitals as we know them today, so people sometimes brought sick relatives to a nearby monastery to be cared for by monks. In addition to monasteries preserving ancient manuscripts, they also preserved the healing arts that had developed in the ancient world. Besides using wine to clean wounds and oil to salve the skin, monks used herbal remedies to address internal ailments. And of course monks would pray for the sick since monasteries were houses of prayer.

When modern medicine began to develop, hospitals and infirmaries were founded by women's religious orders, and in this cultural setting these Catholic institutions were indeed a social sign of divine compassion. This is why nurses in England were addressed as "sister" for decades, even though they were no longer nuns. When men began entering the nursing profession, however, the terminology gradually disappeared.

Sadly, Catholic hospitals in the United States are hardly perceived as sacraments of God's love in today's world. True, they are places of healing, as are all well-run hospitals, and they are places where people can experience compassion and caring from the staff. But as institutions they are often perceived as opponents of fair wages or as antagonistic to women's reproductive health when these issues are reported in the news. Hospitals may be Catholic, but in people's minds they are not always Christian.

Perhaps it is time for the Church to relinquish its attachment to costly health care systems and turn its attention to those who cannot afford health care in America today. The poor often suffer from medical problems that go untreated because they are not severe enough to be brought to an emergency room. Even middle-class people in sparsely populated areas lack basic medical treatment because it is not locally available. In those places, as well as in places of urban poverty, what is needed is not expensive equipment but caring hearts and a healing touch. Medical and dental clinics that offer free or low-cost care for chronic conditions or emergency situations could become the Church's new presence to the poor and needy. In doing so, it would regain the sacramentality that it lost to concern for the latest technology.

BAPTISM

Baptism should be more than joining a club.

Being a member of a club entitles you to certain privileges. Perhaps you can play golf on a private course. Perhaps you can get membership discounts. Perhaps you can get upgrades on car rentals or theater tickets. But you don't have to do anything except enjoy what is unavailable to non-members. All the work is done by the management and staff for the benefit of the members.

For a long time, membership in the Catholic Church was like that. Infants received the sacrament of baptism, giving them the privilege of going to heaven if they died in childhood, the assurance of salvation, and the right to receive additional sacraments when they got older. To remain members in good standing, they needed to attend mass on Sundays, go to confession at least once a year, and obey other church rules. But all of the work was done by the management and staff: the local bishop, the parish pastor, priests, and nuns. Parishioners needed only to pay, pray and obey.

This conception of church dates back to the Middle Ages, when most European Christians were illiterate peasants. It goes without saying that the peasants were not expected to contribute anything to the life of the church.

Indeed, the word "church" came to refer to the clergy, and in particular, to the hierarchy of bishops and cardinals under the pope. When people asked what the Catholic Church teaches, they were asking about teachings that came from the hierarchy.

Even though the Second Vatican Council redefined the meaning of church as the people of God, Catholic institutional life changed very little. At first, the work of the church continued to be performed by clergy and by women in religious orders, and when their numbers began to decline in the 1970s, their work was gradually handed over to laypeople, whether or not they were professionally trained. Through all this, the organizational structure of the church remained the same, with a few ministering to the needs of the many. The many, for the most part, were content to be ministered to and, inevitably, to complain when it was not done well.

In the mean time, the number of non-ministers began to decline, which is another way of saying that they left the church and stopped being counted as Catholics. According to one estimate in the early 2000s, if the non-practicing Catholics in the United States were counted together, they would have comprised the second largest religious body in America, after the Catholic Church.

During the same period, Protestant churches that relied on members to minister to one another grew in size and number. So-called mega-churches grow first by reaching out to non-members and ministering to their needs, and then by inviting them into various forms of ministry within and beyond the congregation.

*

Baptism means immersion.

We don't know why the first followers of Jesus chose ritual immersion to symbolize entrance into the Christian community. By the time the first epistles were written in the 50s, twenty years after Jesus, it was clearly an established practice. Acts of the Apostles describes Peter inviting a crowd to be baptized on the day of Pentecost (Acts 2:38–41), but Acts was written much later than the events described, so we cannot say what actually happened that day. The Gospel According to Matthew portrays the resurrected Christ commanding his followers to baptize people in the name of the Father and of the Son and of the Holy Spirit (Matthew 28: 18–20), but this passage was written in the 80s or 90s, and it probably reflects the late first-century belief that the practice of baptism had divine approval. The actual origins of Christian baptism are lost in history.

Certainly Jesus' cousin John immersed people in water after calling them to reform their lives, but the symbolism of that immersion may have been cleansing or regeneration, and John did not call people into community. Around the time of Jesus, Jews immersed non-Jews who wanted to convert to Judaism as a reminder that the early Israelites had to walk and swim through the Jordan River in order to enter the Promised Land. Perhaps it was this precedent that prompted the first followers of Jesus to immerse non-Jews and Jews alike when they said they wanted to join the early Christian community.

Interestingly, the Greek noun *baptisma*, usually translated as baptism, hardly ever occurs in the New Testament. Much more common is the verb *baptizein*, which meant to immerse, so the noun *baptisma* is more accurately translated as immersion. Once we realize this, and once we remember that proselyte baptism symbolically brought about immersion in the Jewish community and the Jewish way of life (following the Torah and the teachings of the rabbis), then we can see why immersion in water would have been a logical choice for symbolically bringing about immersion in the Christian community and Jesus' way of life.

To be an honest sacrament, therefore, baptism has to entail immersion in the Christian community and in the way of life revealed by Jesus. But for this to happen honestly, the immersion needs to be into a community that is living the way Jesus taught people to live.

*

The Greek word for nice is not found in the New Testament.

People tend to think that being a Christian means being nice. But Jesus never told his followers to be nice, and Paul never wrote to his converts asking them to be nice.

Being nice was a good peasant virtue in medieval times, and being nice is a good middle-class virtue today. We all value being polite and courteous, especially when people disagree. If we cannot see eye-to-eye with others about religion or politics, at least we can be nice to each other and carry on a civil conversation. But Jesus was not crucified for not being nice, and Paul was not martyred because he refused to be nice.

Being nice is not the issue.

Becoming a Christian means being immersed in a community that espouses certain values, and that fosters certain virtues in its members.

In discussions of the sacraments, baptism is customarily treated first because it is a sacrament of initiation into the Christian community. In such discussions, however, the nature of the community is not mentioned except for vague references to the body of Christ or the people of God. In practice, this envisions the church as a club in which members have certain privileges. Once initiated, members do not have to do anything except obey the rules in order to remain a member of the club in good standing.

To counter this customary attitude, we have waited until after we have looked at some of the other sacraments and have seen what they reveal about the Christian community.

From the sacraments of ordination and marriage, we can see that the community values self-giving, service to others, ministering to people's needs, and putting the needs of others ahead of one's own wants. All of this can be summed up in the Greek word, *agápē*, which means caring—caring about and caring for others. It is the word that Jesus uses when he says that the greatest commandments are *agápē* for God and *agápē* for one's neighbor (Matthew 22:37–40 and Mark 12:29–32). It is also the word that he uses when he tells his followers to practice *agápē* toward each other the way he has practiced *agápē* toward them (John 13:34–35).

Clearly, then, Jesus' followers are supposed to be practitioners of *agápē*, people who care about each other and who take care of one another. This value is also manifested in the other two sacramental celebrations already treated, namely, reconciliation and anointing. Reconciliation entails caring about having hurt others and asking their forgiveness, not to mention caring enough to forgive those who have hurt us. The larger dimension of reconciliation, which is reconciliation in society, only comes about when people care enough about their neighborhood or their city to pursue alternatives to incarceration for people who commit crimes. Likewise, anointing of the sick implies caring about the sick, visiting them and comforting them. More broadly, the value of caring that is celebrated in this sacrament can lead to visitation programs, nursing ministries, neighborhood health fairs, and help with paying medical bills.

With these four sacraments in mind, we can say that a community for which they are honest rituals is one that embodies self-giving love, caring for one another and caring about others, one that practices ministry within and beyond the community, one that values marriage not only in the abstract but also by fostering fidelity and long-lasting relationships, one that provides space for reconciliation among members, in families, and beyond the congregation, one that offers healing to members and non-members alike.

*

For baptism to be honest, therefore, the community needs to be practicing the values that are celebrated in its sacraments.

Another way to say this is that the spiritual realities celebrated in its sacramental rituals need to be found in the life of the community and in the lives of its members. Of course, not every member will exemplify every virtue. At the very beginning, Paul recognized that different people bring different gifts to the life of the community (Romans 6:6–8; 1 Corinthians 12–13). No one can do everything, but together all can do what is needed to be a functioning body of Christ energized by God's spirit.

If baptism means immersion into the life of Christ, that life has to be found in the community. Otherwise, there is no life to be immersed in other than the life of a club. The purpose of a club is something other than itself, whether that something else is to be found in the arts or sports, in science or technology. But the purpose of a Christian community is to live the teachings of Jesus and to celebrate the spiritual realities that come into existence when people live that way.

Now, if people are received into a community, it must be living according to values that have not yet been mentioned. Acceptance would be one such value, if those in the community are willing to accept newcomers, especially people who are different from themselves—people of different ages, different races, different nationalities, different economic brackets, and different sexual orientations.

The practice of acceptance reveals the value of belonging, the value of being in a group instead of being alone, the value of relationships overcoming isolation, the value of being in a network of people who care about each other's welfare, the value of knowing that help is available if it is needed. In supportive groups—be they Bible study groups or prayer groups or spirituality groups or therapy groups—people can find a safe environment to grow spiritually, intellectually and morally. They can aslo find the ability to change, if need be.

✶

Making a decision for baptism also implies change.

When Jesus begins his ministry, the usual translation of what he says is, "Repent and believe the good news!" (Mark 1:14). And when Peter preaches to the crowd on Pentecost, he finishes by saying, "Repent and be baptized" (Acts 2:38). The force of these invitations is lost, however, when the Greek word *metanoia* is interpreted as repentance. Repentance has come to mean being sorry for something you've done and promising not to do it again. *Metanoia,* on the other hand, implies a complete change of mind and heart, even adopting a different way of life. Loosely translated, what Jesus says in Mark's gospel is "Change your way of looking at things and believe the good news of how to live differently!" Likewise, what Peter says in Acts could be rendered, "Change your mentality and be immersed in a life-giving community!"

(Why didn't the New Testament writers say this if this is what they meant? It's because they did not have any other words to name what they were referring to. As we saw in chapter two, biblical authors used the words at their disposal to talk about what they and others experienced, but because they did not have a sophisticated vocabulary, words and phrases that they used were later taken to refer to unexperienced metaphysical realities instead of experienced spiritual realities.)

Deciding for baptism therefore means deciding to be immersed in the life of a Christian community. Adults can make this decision for themselves, but parents can also make a decision like this for their children, provided that they themselves are immersed in the life of the community and want to bring their children up in that community.

This may be difficult to imagine. In our own experience, the way churchgoers live is often little different from the way non-churchgoers live. Asking for the baptism of a child, then, does not seem to be asking for a change in values or lifestyle. Suppose, however, that the community in question were Amish. Most people are aware that the Amish lifestyle is very different from the usual American lifestyle. The Amish dress in very plain but practical clothing, they do not use electricity or motorized vehicles, and the men are farmers or craftsmen while the women are child-bearers and home-makers. They live very regimented lives according to a very literalistic reading of the Bible.

For an adult to decide to be Amish would entail an enormous change in mentality, values, and lifestyle. And for parents to decide to immerse their child in an Amish community would be a decision that is palpably different from the usual decision to baptize a child in a Christian community. Yet the decision to be baptized, or to have one's child baptized, ought to feel something like deciding to enter an Amish community. That it does not feel like this is because most Christians do not look weird the way the Amish look weird to outsiders. Most often, they look and behave just like people who are not Christians.

I'll leave it to you to think about why this is the case and what should be done about it, if anything.

*

When Mark Twain was asked if he believed in infant baptism, he replied that he didn't need to believe in it because he'd seen it.

Once the magic and the metaphysics are taken out of baptism, there is no reason why people of any age should be denied baptism. What is important is not someone's age but the presence or absence of the spiritual realities that the ritual refers to, in this case, living the way revealed by Jesus in a community that is doing the same.

The same kind of criterion can be used to address the issue of rebaptism, or going through a baptismal ritual more than once. Catholics, Orthodox and most Protestants do not allow it, either on historical grounds ("It's not our tradition.") or on theological grounds ("The invisible seal of baptism cannot be received more than once."). Evangelicals who reject infant baptism regard being baptized before being old enough to profess faith in Christ as an empty ritual. For them, only believer's baptism is the real thing.

Instead of using ritualistic criteria to approver or disapprove of baptism more than once, the better criterion to use is ritual honesty. Are the spiritual realities being celebrated in the ritual present in those who are participating in the ritual? If so, then it is an authentic baptism because it ritualizes a genuine change in someone's life. It is a real rite of passage. If not, then the externals do not much matter.

Were someone to ask me if I believe in rebaptism, I would have to say I don't have to believe in it. I've seen it.

CONFIRMATION

What does confirmation confirm?

Among Catholic theologians today, there are two theories about confirmation. According to one theory (or theology, since a theology of anything is a religious theory about it), confirmation celebrates a mature acceptance of one's baptismal promises. When someone who was baptized as a child reaches an age where she or he can affirm their faith in a conscious and deliberate way, they bring their baptismal initiation to completion by receiving the sacrament of confirmation. According to the other theology of confirmation, the three sacraments of initiation ought to be received in the proper sequence, which is baptism, then confirmation, then Eucharist. This theory claims that only the fully initiated ought to be admitted to the Eucharist, and therefore children ought to be confirmed before they make their first holy communion.

Both theories are wrong.

The second theory is based on the historical fact that, during the first centuries of Christianity, the ceremonies of initiation were presided over by a bishop who gave his blessing to the new members after the ritual of immersion, thereby confirming their baptism. After this blessing, the new members were allowed to participate in the entire eucharistic liturgy for the very first time in their lives. When they had been catechumens or learners, they had been allowed to hear the scripture readings and listen to the sermon, but they had never been allowed to remain for the part that comes after that, which is called the Liturgy of the Eucharist. Proponents of the second theory argue that in the early church only the fully initiated were admitted to the Eucharist; therefore, only children who are fully initiated should be allowed to receive communion.

There are two flaws in this second theory. The first flaw equates receiving communion with admission to the Liturgy of the Eucharist which includes the distribution of holy communion. But this equation is incorrect. Today, when children make their first communion, they have usually been attending the entire mass, including the Liturgy of the Eucharist, all their lives. So it is incorrect to argue that because converts in the early church

136

were not admitted to the Liturgy of the Eucharist, children today should not be allowed to receive the Eucharist until they are confirmed.

The second flaw in this theory is magical thinking. It is based on the belief that when children are baptized, they *receive* the sacrament of baptism, and that when they are confirmed, they *receive* the sacrament of confirmation. Every Christian should therefore receive both of these sacraments before they are allowed to receive the Blessed Sacrament, which is the body and blood of Christ. In chapter three, however, we were introduced to scholastic sacramental theology, which claimed that when a sacramental ritual is validly performed, a sacramental reality is bestowed on a soul. (This analysis is developed more fully in my scholarly treatment titled *Deconstructing Sacramental Theology and Reconstructing Catholic Ritual*.) The sacramental reality received in baptism was a spiritual seal that marked a person as belonging to Christ, and that enabled the baptized to receive supernatural gifts. According to this theology, in confirmation the baptized received the seven gifts of the Holy Spirit, which enabled Christians to resist temptation and to live courageously good lives as adults. The notion that individuals receive metaphysical realities through religious rituals is an instance of magical thinking. Except for the Eucharist, there are no sacraments that are received during a sacramental ritual.

The first theory presented above, that is, the theology of confirmation according to which the sacrament should not be received until adolescence or early adulthood, is likewise based on magical thinking to the extent that it accepts the medieval belief that the ritual bestows supernatural powers of some sort. Here, the argument suggests that children are not ready to exercise the gifts of the Holy Spirit, so why confer the gifts before they are needed? In addition, proponents of this theory say that the sacrament is an ideal opportunity for young people to accept their baptism and affirm the faith in which they have been raised. Unfortunately, while some adolescents may make a lasting commitment to Christ and the Catholic Church at this time, there is no evidence that confirmation has a noticeable or lasting effect on most of the youngsters who participate in this ceremony. Again, there is an element of magical thinking here in the expectation that the ritual itself should have an effect on people's lives.

What both theologies of confirmation neglect to acknowledge is that the confirmation ritual is a rite of passage. It is not simply an intensification ritual such as a birthday party or anniversary dinner that recognizes something that already exists, or such as Thanksgiving or Independence Day, which does the same on a social level, or such as Christmas or Easter, which does the same in a religious sphere. Celebrations such as these do not make anything happen or change what is already the case, which is why they can take place every year. Any ritual that can be undergone only once, however, is a rite of passage, whether it is an advance in military rank, receiving a diploma or degree, or being inducted into a professional organization.

Structurally, all of the sacraments with the exception of the Eucharist, are rites of passage inasmuch as they change the status of the individuals who go through them—from pagan to Christian, from layman to priest, from single to married, from unforgiven to forgiven, and from unhealed to healed. Sometimes the change in status is permanent, as in the case of baptism, ordination and marriage. If a person can be confirmed only once (or receive the sacrament only once, according to the scholastic theology), then confirmation is a rite of passage.

The problem with both of the theologies of confirmation in vogue to-day is that they accept that the children or adolescents who are confirmed do not change their status in the church. Children who are confirmed before first communion are no different than children who are not confirmed first, and adolescents who are confirmed in high school are no different than adolescents who are not confirmed. They have the same standing in the community that they had before the ceremony, which is to say that they are still regarded as children or as adolescents.

For an institution to maintain that a sacrament is a rite of passage when it makes no real difference in the lives of people is intellectually dishonest. The only change that actually happens when young people are confirmed today is a change in sacramental record keeping. Once they are confirmed, there is a record of it, so they cannot go through the ceremony again.

*

How, then, could confirmation be made an honest sacrament?

First, whichever transition the ceremony is intended to facilitate and celebrate, the ceremony must mark a genuine transition in a person's life. There must be a *before* and *after*, a *from* and a *to*, in the life of the partici-pant. The person's life has to be different after the ceremony from the way it was before. This usually entails having greater responsibilities and more rights than the person had before.

Second, in order to maintain the sacrament's traditional connection with baptism, the ritual could celebrate a deepening of one's baptismal commitment or of one's immersion in the life of the Christian community. Especially in a cultural setting where infant or child baptism is retained, it could mark a transition into a deeper personal commitment or a broader involvement with the life of the community.

Third, although all would be invited to become more deeply immersed in the life of the community through ministering within the community or on its behalf, this would not be a celebration that is extended to all, as confirmation is today. There are valid reasons why individuals might not be able to take this further step into community involvement.

Fourth, a transition that is worth ritualizing could be something like entering into a form of unordained ministry, such as a professional position in a parish or a position of greater responsibility in a community. Currently, bishops and pastors are ceremonially installed, and while such ceremonies are not sacraments in the traditional sense, they are transition rituals that celebrate and effect a person's passage into a new set of responsibilities and rights. There is no reason why pastoral administrators, youth ministers, music directors and the like could not enter their office with a public ceremony that introduces them to the community and in which they receive, in some fashion, the community's blessing.

Fifth, groups of individuals might ceremonially enter their ministry through such a rite of passage. This would be analogous to what is sometimes called a commissioning service. It could involve prayers, readings, blessings, words from community leaders or from those entering into ministry, and adaptations of secular rituals such as applause.

Sixth, since this reinterpretation of confirmation does not include the idea of an invisible seal or mark on the soul, there is no reason why this ceremony could not be repeated. Indeed, if a person moved from one unordained ministry to another, each move would be celebrated in a new ceremony. And if a person dropped out of active involvement in church life for a while and later wanted to reenter it, such a return and reentrance could be publicly celebrated.

Seventh, such ceremonies need not be stand-alone rituals, but they could be additions to or insertions in a eucharistic liturgy, following the example set by healing services or communal anointings set in the context of a mass.

EUCHARIST

Lastly, there is the eucharistic liturgy, commonly called the mass.

The word, "eucharist," comes from a Greek verb, *eucharistein*, meaning to give thanks. At Jesus' last supper, he gave thanks before giving special significance to the bread and wine he passed to his disciples. It was customary at the time to offer a prayer of thanks to God before and during a meal. Acts of the Apostles mentions three occasions when the early followers of Jesus gathered to break bread together (see Acts 2, 20 and 27), and Paul refers to the Christian practice of the Lord's supper in 1 Corinthians 11.

By the second century, the weekly practice of eating together was called a giving of thanks (*eucharistia*), and even the symbolic foods of bread and wine were called the thanksgiving (*eucharistia*). Two centuries later, when the weekly supper evolved into a lengthy ritual of public worship, *eucharistia* had become a proper name, so that the worship service was itself called eucharist or eucharistic liturgy.

Because it has not changed much since the fourth century, you can get a glimpse of Sunday worship in the patristic era by attending the weekly liturgy in any Eastern Orthodox church or any Eastern Rite Catholic church. Worship in the Western or Latin church, however, changed quite drastically after the fall of the Roman Empire. Mainly, it became simpler and shorter, much like the low mass said in Latin before the Second Vatican Council.

By the Middle Ages, the word *eucharistia* had become the name of the consecrated bread and wine, also known as the body and blood of Christ, and the worship service itself came to be called *missa* or mass. The origins of the term *missa* are lost in history, but it may have come from the dismissal at the end of the service, when the priest said, "*Ite, missa est.*" In Latin, the words meant, "Go, it is sent," referring to the consecrated bread that was being sent to shut-ins, but the same words could also be taken to mean, "Go, it is the mass," meaning that the mass is finished. Because the consecrated elements were understood to be Christ himself under the appearance of bread and wine, they were called the Blessed Sacrament or the Eucharist, the names being capitalized because they referred to a divine person.

For the medieval schoolmen, then, there were seven sacraments, six of which were rituals and one which was a spiritual reality that was brought into being when a priest said the words, "This is my body. . . . This is my blood," over bread and wine during a mass.

*

The mass in the Middle Ages was regarded as a sacrifice.

In the late first century, a Christian document referred to the meal shared by Christians as a sacrifice, *thusia* in Greek. In the ancient world, devout pagans would gather in a temple to share a festive meal in the presence of their god, represented by a statue or some other image. In the second century, a Palestinian Christian named Justin argued that the Christian sacrifice had replaced Jewish sacrifices in fulfillment of an Old Testament prophesy. By Justin's time, there were Christians in all parts of the Roman Empire, and he took this text to refer to his own religion:

> Everywhere a pure sacrifice is offered to my name because my name is great among the nations, says the Lord almighty. (Malachi 1:11)

A "pure sacrifice" in the ancient world was a religious meal shared by individuals who were ritually pure. Some of the food was offered to a god, some was offered to the temple priests, and the rest was consumed by the attendees. Since this was similar to what the followers of Jesus did during their weekly gatherings, Justin and others used this similarity to argue that Christians should not be accused of atheism just because they did not gather in temples for their sacrifices.

Centuries later, when the full meal had evolved into a symbolic meal of bread and wine, the concept of sacrifice was still applied to Christian worship, but the meaning shifted. Instead of the emphasis being placed on the sacred meal, it was put on the sacred food, which was also called a sacrifice. The Greek *thusia* was translated into the Latin *sacrificium*, literally something made sacred. The sacred food, in the minds of Christians who had never attended a pagan sacrifice, was the body and blood of Christ.

This was the concept of sacrifice that was inherited by the schoolmen in the Middle Ages. The ritual performed by priests in Latin was understood to be a sacrifice, not in the sense of being a sacred meal, but in the sense of food being offered to God. Christ's death on the cross was interpreted as the sacrificial offering of God the Son to God the Father, and the mass was therefore a re-presentation of that sacrifice in which devout Christians could spiritually join themselves with Christ in offering themselves to God.

Using this mistaken understanding of sacrifice, medieval theologians misinterpreted the quotation from Malachi, cited above. Christ, who was sinless, was taken to be the pure sacrifice spoken of by the prophet.

*

The mass is not a sacrifice in either of these senses.

Certainly it is not a festive meal, except by analogy. There is no real food, except for bread and wine, and for centuries, only the priest was allowed to partake of the sacred wine, lest some of it spill. This has changed since Vatican II, but most Catholics still use tasteless communion wafers called hosts.

Lamenting the Church's strict rules about the ingredients in a host, one liturgist observed that it is sometimes easier to believe that it's the body of Christ than to believe that it's bread.

Nor is the mass a sacrifice in the medieval scholastic sense, even though Catholics spoke about "the holy sacrifice of the mass" during the Tridentine era and up to the Second Vatican Council. Catholics who attended the Latin mass were told to believe that during the most important part of the service, Christ was made present on the altar and offered to God for their salvation. This was not a repetition of Christ's sacrifice on the cross but a way of making the reality of that saving act present for all who were disposed to prayerfully enter that sacred moment. In a sense, the mass was a way that devout Catholics could be spiritually present at Calvary, and join with Christ's sacrifice for the salvation of the world. Thus, his self-sacrifice became their own self-sacrifice.

While the mass might have been this type of religious ritual for centuries, it no longer is. Although some of the prayers in the revised text refer to what is happening as a sacrifice, there is usually too much going on for people to enter into a prayerful attitude of self-surrender to God. Even though there is no music or singing during the Eucharistic Prayer, during which the consecration of the elements takes place, the prayer is relatively short and it ends with an acclamation in which the people sing, "Amen!" After a few more prayers said by the priest, all say the Lord's Prayer, and this is followed by the distribution of holy communion, during which a hymn is usually sung. In such a busy liturgy there is literally no opportunity to enter into the sacred space of Calvary and the sacred time of Christ's death. I would venture to wager that no one leaves a Catholic mass today feeling that they have been present at a sacrifice, or that they have offered themselves in sacrifice during the service.

✳

If the mass is a celebration, what does it celebrate?

Liturgists sometimes talk about celebrating the liturgy, but when you think about it, this does not make sense. A celebration does not celebrate itself. A birthday party does not celebrate a birthday party, and Independence Day fireworks do not celebrate Independence Day fireworks.

A celebration always celebrates something other than itself. It celebrates something that it refers to. It has a referent. A birthday party refers to someone being a year older. An Independence Day celebration refers to our country's independence. If we were under foreign rule, there would be nothing to celebrate.

✳

All formal rituals are celebrations of one sort or another.

Rites of passage or transition rituals celebrate changes that are happening in people's lives at the same time that they facilitate those changes and make them happen. A commencement exercise celebrates the completion of an extended education effort and the beginning of a new stage in life. A wedding celebrates the love two people have for one another and the beginning of a life together. An inauguration into public office celebrates and initiates a person into public service.

Intensification rituals, on the other hand, celebrate social realities that are important in people's lives. A birthday party does not make anyone a year older, but it celebrates someone's life and, by extension, the relationships between that person and the people at the party. Christmas does not give birth to Jesus, and Easter does not make him rise from the dead; they and other religious feasts celebrate events that are important for Christians. A Thanksgiving dinner does not make anything new happen, but it celebrates family and other close relationships.

✳

Thanksgiving is an important clue. Eucharist originally meant thanksgiving.

Even though the mass is no longer a meal, let's think about meals for a moment. Not meals taken alone, but meals shared with others. Not business lunches, but lunches taken as a break from work. Not formal banquets with a bunch of strangers, but meals taken with people you know.

You probably like the people you eat with, that is, the people you choose to eat with. (Siblings around the dinner table may not qualify here.) If you are eating in a school cafeteria, you probably have something in common with your table mates. At a certain level, eating lunch together is a celebration of what you have in common and, probably, your friendship with each other. Something similar is usually true of people who work in the same office or factory, and who have lunch with the same group every day. Sharing what's been going on at home, complaining about the boss, talking about your latest aches and pains—these are all mini-rituals that reinforce your connections to your co-workers and celebrate your relationships with one another. Going to a restaurant for a date celebrates the beginning of a relationship, its continuance, and your hopes for its future. Family meals are less common that they used to be, but in obvious and subtle ways they celebrate being a family.

OK, so you don't get to eat a lot when you come to mass, but you do some of the other things that people do when they get together for a meal. Most importantly, they show up. Next, they greet the people they know and sometimes people they don't know. Third, they bring their experiences and feelings and ideas with them. Fourth, they have some things in common: they share the same religious faith, or they live in the same part of town, or they are on committees together, or they have kids in the parish school or sports teams, or they share a similar ethnic heritage, or they get spiritually rejuvenated, or they like the music, or they enjoy the preaching, or any combination of these. What they have in common may be any number of things, but if they had nothing in common, they would not all be in the same place at the same time.

The people at mass (or a service in any other religion, for that matter) each have their own individual lives, but their lives also intersect to a greater or lesser extent. They have lives apart, but they also share life together for some part of the week between Sundays. They have at least some things in common, and they are aware of those things at some level when they get together. Even if they contribute nothing else to the parish, they put something in the collection basket when it comes around. It is a symbolic gesture that says, "I support what is going on here and I want it to continue."

In other words, "I am thankful for it."

*

Does the mass have a single meaning?

In chapter one, we saw that the meaning that is commonly attributed to words and symbols is actually in people's minds. If this is true of a single word, then it is also true of a sentence, a paragraph, a chapter and a book. Although critics and professors can make money telling people what a book means, what they are actually doing is putting marks on a page or making sounds in the air that readers and listeners may find meaningful. The readers and listeners in turn may keep these meanings or ideas in mind when they turn to the actual book and begin the process of interpreting what they find on the pages. A complex novel can mean different things to different readers, and the same book may mean something to a young reader who, years later, might read the book again and find it meaningful is a different way. One definition of a classic is a work that people continue to find meaningful over a great length of time. The words on the page do not change, but the interpreters change and the novel still speaks to them, as it were.

A form of art that is totally wordless is symphonic music. A concerto or a symphony is, so to speak, all symbol, or a long concatenation of sounds in need of interpretation. In a concert hall, some people might find it meaningful and some might not. Ordinary listeners who do find it meaningful might be hard pressed to put the meaning into words, but music critics develop the skill of listening to a piece of music and talking about it in a meaningful way. A concert is a good example of how a performance can mean different things to different people because it is impossible to point to the music score and argue that the meaning of the piece is there on the paper.

Any eucharistic liturgy is a symbolic performance that is in need of interpretation by those who are present at it. Theologians may write articles and books about *the* meaning of the mass, and experts in spirituality may write about what *the* mass should mean to devout Catholics. But *the* mass is an abstraction. No one ever attends *the* mass; people are always present at this mass or that mass.

At best, *the* eucharistic liturgy or mass is a text, a liturgical text, a script that contains directions about what should be said and done by the presider and the people at different points when the script is performed. Any actual mass, however, is a liturgical performance that occurs at a certain place and time. The actual meaning, therefore, of any eucharistic liturgy is the meaning, or more likely, the collection of meanings that it has for the people in attendance.

✶

Consider the possibility that any mass celebrates the life of the people doing the celebrating.

Let's say you are in a restaurant, seated near a long table where people are celebrating a couple's golden wedding anniversary. It would not be far fetched to imagine that the celebration means some things to the couple ("We really made it!" "The kids actually remembered and organized this!"), some things to their adult children ("They put up with a lot when they were raising us!" "I'm so glad this finally came together."), other things to the grandchildren ("They are really old!" "I love seeing Grandma and Grandpa!"), and still something else to you, the onlooker.

Each of those in attendance at this ritual brings their own life experience to the ritual and uses that life experience to find meaning in the event. Here there is no script, no text and no written instructions. Like a musical performance, if people find meaning in it, they must bring something to the celebration that enables them to feel, understand and appreciate it from their own perspective.

In a similar way, a community's liturgy is meaningful because people bring a multiplicity of meanings to it. To the extent that it is truly a celebration and not the fulfillment of an obligation, it is an opportunity to feel more deeply the feelings that bring them to church and the values they find in being a member of the community. The eucharistic liturgy is an intensification ritual that is not intended to change anyone the way a rite of passage does. It is a chance, presented once a week or more, to remember and affirm what brings people together into this particular community.

No one can celebrate everything that is going on in the community, since no one (not even the pastor) knows everything that is going on. But everyone celebrates their part of what goes on in the parish—taking the parish as typical of a Catholic community, even though there are others, such as communities of monks or nuns. For some, it may be what is going on in their personal life—their prayer life or their spiritual life. For others, it may be what is going on in the life of a group—the parents' club, the soccer team, the scout troop, the Bible study group, the soup kitchen or the neighborhood pantry. Their involvement may also be in groups that enhance the life of the community, for instance, the finance committee, the worship committee, the social committee, the evangelization committee, the music ensemble, the choir, or the parish council. A few, such as the pastor and the parish staff, may even have a sense of the whole, for which they are thankful and in response to which they celebrate.

*

It should not surprise us that the mass has many meanings.

Catholics use the mass to celebrate birth, death, and many things in between. The sacramental rites of baptism, confirmation, marriage and ordination are relatively short, so they are almost always augmented and surrounded by a eucharistic liturgy. A Catholic funeral is almost always preceded by what used to be called a requiem mass and is now called a mass of Christian burial. Even the anointing of the sick can be set in the context of a eucharistic liturgy if a large number of people are to be anointed.

In addition, Catholic institutions use the mass to celebrate the beginning and end of the school year, special saints' days, events in the life of Christ besides those in the liturgical calendar, institutional anniversaries and wedding anniversaries. The arrival of a new pastor or a new bishop is always celebrated with a mass.

When attending such events, I suspect that most people in attendance do not pay much attention to the words of the rite, except perhaps during the consecration of the bread and wine, because this part of the ceremony is done with great solemnity, and because Catholics have been taught that this is the moment when bread and wine are changed into the body and blood of Christ. People with a special devotion to Christ in the Eucharist may find this moment deeply meaningful, but for most Catholics it is something that must be done so that holy communion can be distributed to those in attendance.

*

Underneath it all, there are spiritual realities.

Chapter one introduced the concept of spiritual realities, things that are real but not material, things that are present in people's lives and that make them meaningful.

We talked about love in the sense of caring, commitment in the sense of self-giving, and ministry in the sense of meeting the needs of others. We also talked about community, acceptance, belonging, strengthening and healing, forgiveness and fidelity. These are all values that are found in people's lives and make life worth living. They are also principles that direct people's actions and affect their behavior. These are spiritual realities that are acknowledged and celebrated in the seven traditional sacraments.

Moreover, part of every eucharistic liturgy are readings from the Bible. These readings present stories and instructions about a wide variety of spiritual realities that can be highlighted in homilies and elaborated in sermons. The worth of every person, the beauty of creation, the presence of mystery, God's love for all, compassion for the sick, justice for the oppressed, acceptance of those who are different, hope in the face of adversity, responsibility and courage, honor and truth, the meaningfulness of life, risk-taking and conversion, hope beyond the grave—these are all spiritual realities that the scriptures talk about and that need to be part of people's lives if they are to be meaningful.

These are also spiritual realities that need to permeate our culture for there to be a livable world and a society in which people's needs can be met, their individuality honored, their differences respected, their opportunities enhanced, and their potential realized. They are spiritual realities that need to be promoted in schools, in the arts, in the media, and in public institutions such as the legislature and the judiciary.

Much of contemporary culture, however, glorifies and promotes wealth and power, winners over losers, sexual satisfaction and sensual gratification, the accumulation of stuff, and many other forms of addictive behavior. In the midst of this, there needs to be an institution that is counter-cultural and that ritualizes spiritual realities that are life-giving and life-enhancing.

For many, that institution is the Catholic Church. But for any church to bring about the kingdom of God on earth today, it needs to move beyond doctrines and beliefs. It needs to do what Jesus teaches and celebrate what's real.

According to traditional theology, the eucharistic liturgy celebrates the paschal mystery, or the death and resurrection of Christ.

This is usually taken to refer to something that happened long ago and far away. In this way of looking at it, Christians celebrate the fact that Jesus Christ lived and died about two thousand years ago in what is now Israel and Palestine. His humanity incarnated the word of God, so when he spoke, God spoke through him. His death atoned for the sins of humanity past and future, and his resurrection showed that God had accepted his sacrifice. Therefore he was raised from the dead and is now at the right hand of God.

That's the way the story goes, but most attempts to explain it fall short.

Most theories are variations of an explanation first proposed by Anselm of Canterbury in the Middle Ages. He envisioned God the Father as a medieval monarch whose honor was offended when Adam and Eve (at that point, the entirety of humanity) sinned against him in the Garden of Eden. Since God is an infinite being, their sin was an infinite offense against his honor, and no finite act of reparation could atone for it. So God the Son mercifully took on human flesh in order to satisfy divine justice, which demanded reparation equal to the offense. Being divine, Christ's death on the cross was of infinite merit, satisfying the demands of divine justice and restoring the honor of God the Father.

Besides casting God the Father as an intransigent deity, demanding full restitution for the violation of his honor, such explanations do not explain why the Son had to die such a brutal death. Every good deed of the divine Son would have been of infinite merit, according to this line of reasoning, and so a painful death was not necessary. Moreover, an explanation such as this makes little sense today, when most Christians envision God as a loving father, as depicted in the parable of the Prodigal Son, rather than an aloof monarch demanding that justice be satisfied.

Such are the perils of turning scriptural metaphors into metaphysical realities. Some stories ultimately resist translation into scientific categories. Christ's reparation for sins works well as a story, and in the hands of a great preacher, it can bring people to tears. But intellectually, it makes no logical sense.

The story of Jesus' death and resurrection is a myth in the sense described in chapter four. It is a story that is always true rather than a story that was true at a certain place and time. It is a story in which people can situate their lives and that can tell people how to live. It is a story that helps people to make sense of the world and make sense of what is happening to them.

This important teaching in Christianity is sometimes referred to as the paschal mystery, referencing the Jewish feast of *Pesach* or Passover, the time of year when Jesus died. The name evokes images of the first Passover, when the angel of death passed over the homes of the Israelites, marked with the blood of the paschal lamb, on its way to kill the first-born of every family in Egypt. The paschal mystery is the mystery of how the death and resurrection of Jesus brought salvation to humanity.

Taken literally, the story is impossible to explain. This is sometimes why it is called a mystery: we just cannot understand it. It is interpreted as analogous to the mystery of death and rebirth in the cycle of the seasons: in winter, things die, and in spring, they are born again. Or it is interpreted as analogous to death and life in the cycle of generations: the old die, but children are born.

In most European languages, the Christian feast is called *Pascha* or some other variant of *Pesach*. In English, however, the feast is called Easter, after Ēostre, a Germanic goddess of spring. Hence the bunnies and chicks on Easter cards.

Homilies and sermons usually interpret the paschal mystery as one in which the participants are passive. Vegetation dies in the winter and is reborn in the spring; the plants do not have to do anything but wait until they come to life again. In the human cycle, the death of loved ones brings a period of grieving, after which life can once again resume. Analogously, Christ died for us, and because of his resurrection, we too can be reborn. We need only accept it on faith.

While it is true that death and rebirth are a mystery, it is not the Christian mystery. It is a secular mystery, known to anyone who has observed the cycle of the seasons or the cycle of life. Known for centuries to pagans in Europe, it is the mystery that gave us the name, Easter.

The paschal mystery, however, is the one that Jesus lived and invited his disciples to discover by living it. Sell what you own and give the money to the poor, and come follow me. Love your neighbor as yourself. The greatest love is dedicating your life to those you care about. Take care of each other the way I have taken care of you.

Most of us have participated in this mystery. It's what happens when we get up in the middle of the night to calm a crying baby. It's what happens when we go to work every day to feed our family. It's what happens when we help our kids with their homework instead of watching television. It's what happens when we stop to help someone with a flat tire. It's what we experience many times when we choose to serve others—as teachers and nurses and counselors and social workers—as our life's work. It's what we experience when we are members of a service organization in our church or town. It's what we experience when we become involved in making the world a better place through political involvement. We give of ourselves and, mysteriously, our life is enriched by doing so.

This, then, is the good news. The way to truly live is to live for others. The way to a rich life is to give your life away. The way to endless vitality is *agápē*. The early Christian movement was called simply The Way (Acts 9:2).

The eucharistic liturgy, then, is how Christians thank God that Jesus has shown them the way to live. But it is honest thanks only when people are honestly trying to live that way.

Conclusion

IN THIS ANALYSIS OF sacraments and sacramentality, I have prescribed no norms except one, namely, honesty. Honest rituals celebrate what is actually happening in people's lives. Dishonest rituals fail to do this, usually by celebrating some mythical events or some metaphysical realities that are believed to exist.

This is generally the way it is in Christianity and in my branch of it, which is Roman Catholicism. Having studied and taught about world religions, I would venture to say that this is the case in all the major religions of humanity.

Certainly, Christian rituals would have to celebrate values and principles that have been revealed in the New Testament, especially in the life and teachings of Jesus Christ. To be honest, such rituals should celebrate such values and principles, not in the abstract, but as they are found in the actual lives of individuals and communities.

How this is done, however, ought to be left to the creativity and judgment of those who are responsible for designing church rituals and implementing their performance. In the global Catholic community, this would most likely be local conferences of bishops.

In this book, I have suggested how the traditional seven sacraments might be re-imagined and redesigned in a culturally Western context. But there is no reason why Christian and Catholic rituals could not look very different in non-Western communities. Native Americans on both the northern and southern continents have their own ceremonial styles, as do the many peoples of the Middle East, Africa and Asia.

What would unify such rituals and make them symbolic expressions of the Christian faith would be the spiritual realities that they celebrate— conversion and community, acceptance and belonging, commitment and fidelity, healing and strengthening, forgiveness and reconciliation, service and self-giving, love in the sense of caring for others, and the spiritual transformation that results from living according to the gospel.

Beyond that, there are no limits.

Suggested Reading

Since many of the ideas in this book are new, even for people who think and write about sacraments and rituals, there are not many titles to recommend as background reading. I shall, however, tell you about some of the books you may find helpful for understanding this book.

The first is *Deconstructing Sacramental Theology and Reconstructing Catholic Ritual* (Wipf and Stock, 2015), which is the longer and more scholarly version of the ideas presented in this book. If you want proof of the claims made in this book about the historical relativity of Catholic sacramental doctrines, you will find it in that book.

The second is *The Sacraments: An Interdisciplinary and Interactive Study* (Liturgical Press, 2009) and its accompanying website, www.The-Sacraments.org. Both are by me, and they will give you an introduction to understanding sacraments as symbolic rituals that are given religious explanations by theologians and liturgists.

The third is *Christianity Rediscovered* (Orbis Books, 2003) by Vincent Donovan and first published in 1978, describing Donovan's experiences as a missionary in Africa. What he learned about indigenous rituals helped me to understand how rituals are expressions of experienced spiritual realities.

None of my books could have been written if I had not read and appropriated *Insight: A Study in Human Understanding* (Longmans, 1957) by Bernard Lonergan. If you find that work impenetrable, you may want to read other books and articles about Lonergan's cognitional theory, which provides the philosophical foundation for this book.

As a student in the sixties and seventies, I was much impressed with the work of Marshall McLuhan. If you read *The Gutenberg Galaxy* (University of Toronto Press, 1962) and *Understanding Media* (Sphere Books, 1967), you will get a sense of how culture and technology affect how we perceive and think.

For insights into our contributions to the world that we live in, read *The Social Construction of Reality* by Peter Berger and Thomas Luckman (Doubleday, 1966). Subtitled *A Treatise in the Sociology of Knowledge*, it will help you understand how meanings found in many minds get assumed to be objectively true.

More recently, *Lay Spirituality: From Traditional to Postmodern* (Wipf and Stock, 2017) by Pierre Hégy substantiates the idea that for many people today, the meaningfulness of their religious practices is more connected to their individual and social experiences than it is to traditional doctrines.

Made in the USA
San Bernardino, CA
22 January 2018